The
RICHER LIFE
SYSTEM

The
RICHER LIFE SYSTEM

Create Your Best Life—
One Simple Choice
at a Time

ZIG ZIGLAR

MEDIA

Published 2022 by Gildan Media LLC
aka G&D Media
www.GandDmedia.com

FIRST EDITION 2022

Front cover design by David Rheinhardt of Pyrographx

Design by Meghan Day Healey of Story Horse, LLC

Library of Congress Cataloging-in-Publication Data is available upon request

ISBN: 978-1-7225-0512-7

10   9   8   7   6   5   4   3   2   1

Contents

Preface

Someone once said, "One picture is worth 10,000 words."

But if you think about it, that individual never really read the Twenty-third Psalm, the Bill of Rights, or the Lord's Prayer, or understood all of the beauties and benefits that can be communicated with the simple spoken words "I love you."

I don't believe that one picture is worth 10,000 words. I believe that words are the most potent weapons we have in our entire arsenal. We can use words to move ourselves and others into a happier, more productive, and more fulfilled life.

This book is going to be an exciting event in your life—or should I say series of events? I'll be talking about how you can get the things that you really want, and, in my mind, deserve.

This book is about you, your family, your future, and how you can get more out of all of them by giving more to each of them. It's the end—or the beginning of the end—of negative thinking, negative action, and negative reaction. It's the end of being influenced by little people with little minds, thinking little thoughts about the trivia that is the stock and trade of Mr. and Mrs. Mediocrity. In short, this book is the end for you of the world's most deadly disease: hardening of the attitudes.

1

What Do You Really Want?

The first purpose of this course is to open your mind, stir your imagination, arouse your curiosity, and create dissatisfaction with your status quo. The second purpose is to identify the things you want in life and chart a course of action to get them. The third purpose is to arouse the sleeping giant inside you. The fourth purpose is to help you recognize and overcome your loser's limp. I will tell many stories, because I believe stories are life itself.

Here's the first one. I was flying in from Chicago on the plane one evening, and I was seated next to an old boy. I couldn't help noticing that he had his wedding band on the index finger of his left hand. I said, "Friend, you've got your wedding band on the wrong finger."

He laughed and said, "Yeah. I married the wrong woman."

Of course, I have no idea whether this man married the wrong woman or not, but I do believe that many people have wrong ideas about what life has to offer.

I'm convinced that life today offers more privileges, more opportunities, and more benefits than it has ever done in the history of humankind. I'm going to suggest that everything that you want in life is available—money, health, happiness, peace of mind, security, opportunity.

You may be amazed to see that I listed money first, but I don't think you need to be. I don't think there's anything wrong with having money. As a matter of fact, I believe that people don't have more money simply because they don't understand it.

You'd be amazed at the people that still talk about cold, hard cash. It's neither cold nor hard. It's soft and warm and very comfortable, and it has such a magnificent color. I don't know if you've ever noticed this or not, but the color of money blends with every other color in existence. I find no conflict anywhere. It goes perfectly with red or blue or yellow or polka dot. I've also discovered that the more money you've got, the better it goes with whatever else you might happen to have.

Occasionally, I hear somebody say, "I don't want to make a lot of money," but I believe that a man or woman who would make a statement like that will lie about other things too.

Throughout this book, I'll be talking a lot about money, but in a different light from usual. I'm going to emphasize one point, as I've done many times: you can get everything in life that you want if you will just help enough other people get what they want.

I believe money is a yardstick. It cannot be our god. If you make money your god, then you're in trouble, because the Bible tells us, "He that loveth silver shall not be satisfied with silver; nor he that loveth abundance with increase" (Ecclesiastes 5:10).

When billionaire H. L. Hunt died, somebody asked, "I wonder how much money old man Hunt really left." Somebody else said, "He left it all."

No, you can't let money become your god. Yet at the same time, I believe you're morally obligated to earn as much money as you legitimately and honestly can, because this is the way to render a great deal more service to your fellow man. If you earn money under the right principles, it is a magnificent thing to have.

Furthermore, I don't know what your experience has been, but I've both had money and haven't had it, and it is better to have it. Just don't let it be your god. Get as much money as you want, but don't ever let it get you, because the moment it does is the moment when you've got too much.

I'm also going to talk about peace of mind. I do not believe that we can have complete peace of mind until we have once and for all resolved the question of eternity. Once you've got that settled, the other things tend to be fairly easy. Peace of mind comes naturally when you can go to bed knowing that you don't have to worry about anything all night long, because the Lord will be up all night anyhow, and when you don't have to worry about tomorrow because even though we do not know what tomorrow holds, we know Who holds tomorrow.

I will also talk about health, both physical and mental. As a matter of fact, there are three times as many people in hospitals for emotional disturbances than there are for physical disturbances. They're suffering from what I call "stinkin' thinkin'." One purpose of this book is to give you a thorough checkup from the neck up because if we can do that, we'll eliminate many of the problems that people have in life.

I'll also talk about physical health, because I believe it's important to be physically healthy. At one point in my life, I lost thirty-seven pounds. But the only thing I'm really going to tell you about dieting is, stay away from cottage cheese. This is not necessarily scientific, but over the years I have become convinced that cottage cheese must be the most fattening food in existence. That's because I don't see anyone but fat folks eating it. So by law of elimination, stay away from cottage cheese.

I'm going to talk about happiness as well. I believe that happiness is an inside job. I fervently believe that you will have much more happiness if you help enough other people get what they want, because I don't believe you can make somebody else happy without having a great deal of it rub off on you.

I'm also going to be talking about security, which is an inside job too. Security is not in the job. Security is in the individual. It's what you do with and how you see what you've got. It's how you react to other people and other conditions.

I believe that all of these things—health, wealth, and happiness—are available. Now I've got to confess that I'm an optimist. You know what an optimist is? A fella who, when he wears his shoes out, just figures he's back on his feet.

Let me see if can explain why I'm optimistic. The Bible clearly tells me that the Lord has forgiven me for everything I've done in the past. That brings me right up to date. Jesus Christ said that he's come that you might have life and that you might have it more abundantly (John 10:10). That takes care of the present. John 3:16 says I'm going to be with him forever, and the Twenty-third Psalm says I'm going to live in his house. Now with the facilities of the universe at his disposal, I've got an idea that it's going to be some place. And I can't believe he wants me in a chicken shack between here and there.

So with my past forgiven, my present assured, and my future irrevocably guaranteed, tell me: what in the world have I got to be negative about? I'm not relying on the wisdom of man. I'm relying on the power of Almighty God. And I believe that he's given us a lot of power, and if we properly use it, amazing things will happen.

Now you may say, "Zig, all that sounds pretty good, but maybe I don't have the same beliefs that you do, so can you give me any advice?" Yep, sure can.

I believe you can get health, wealth, and happiness, but only if you build a proper foundation. In the first place, I believe you've got to be honest. It has nothing to do with paying your credit cards or telephone bills or making your house payments when they're due. It has nothing to do with making certain the check is good when you write it. That has no bearing whatever on honesty. In today's communications complex, when you can write a bad check in Dallas on Monday and they'll know about it in Portland, Oregon, on Monday afternoon, I think writing a bad check is very foolish. That has nothing to do with honesty.

Honesty is what you do in the dark. Honesty is the way you deal with yourself. Honesty is looking at things in such a manner that you know what you're saying and doing is exactly right.

If you're going to get the things in life that you want, you've got to build your character. When you see a building being constructed, you can look at the site and tell how high the building is going to be by the depth of the hole. You can tell the size of the business by the solidness of the organization or the management team. You've got to have a foundation. I believe character is a foundation.

And, yes, you've got to have faith. Once a young man said he couldn't believe in anything he couldn't see. I said, "How about turning the lights on? It's kind of dark in here." He reached over and flipped the lights on.

"Why'd you do that?" I asked.

"Well, you wanted more light."

"Let me ask you: what do you know about electricity?"

"Nothing."

"Then why did you flip the switch?"

"I wanted light."

"How'd you know the light was going to be there? You didn't, but in faith you flipped it on."

We flip the switch in faith. I don't know anything about electricity, but I'll get as much light out of the bulb as the most accomplished electrician who ever lived. All I've got to do is flip the switch.

You know, it's a funny thing. We drive 3,000 miles. We pull into a strange service station, buy an unknown brand of gasoline, pumped into the tank by a guy we've never seen before and never will see again. Our entire mobility depends on the fact that that is gasoline and not buttermilk, yet we say, "Fill her up." With faith, we do exactly the same thing.

We go to the grocery store and we buy milk in a carton we've never seen, in a grocery store we've never been in, which got it from a dairy they know nothing about. But in faith we buy the milk, and we drink it.

We do not have to know and understand everything in order to have faith. We ride down the highway and see a pasture. We see cows and sheep and chickens eating grass. The cow takes the grass and gives milk, the sheep takes the grass and grows wool, and the chicken takes the grass and lays an egg. So far I have never had somebody say to me, "I'm not going to eat that egg, because I don't understand how that chicken takes that grass and makes an egg out of it." Neither does science—some of the most brilliant people in the world. But in faith, we accept those things.

If we're going to get the things that we really want, we also have to have loyalty and integrity. All of these qualities represent the foundation stones; if you compromise on any of them, if you take any shortcuts anywhere down the line, you might end up with a lot of money but a stomach full of ulcers. You might go to the top of the corporate ladder, but you might lose your family along the way. And I don't believe that the man or woman is successful who sacrifices those things along the way. But I believe health, wealth, and happiness are all available if we have the right principles, if we build on the right foundation.

At this point, some people might not have all of the characteristics they might like to have, but I believe that we can and must develop those qualities along the way. I'd have to lift weights to develop muscles, wouldn't I?

In one of my books, there is an illustration of an elevator to the top. It had a sign on it, which said, "Out of Order."

The elevator to the top is out of order, it's always been out of order, and it always will be out of order. You've got to take the stairs, and you're going to have to take them one at a time.

Once my wife, son, and I visited the Washington Monument. As we gathered around it, the line was enormous. Everybody was waiting to catch the elevator. But I noticed a little sign that said, "There's no waiting to get to the top if you're willing to take the stairs."

That's the message that I want to get across in this book: there is no waiting to get to the top if you're willing to do your part.

Some say, "Zig, I have honesty, I have character, I have loyalty, I have integrity, and I have faith, but I'm still broke. How do you explain that?"

Let me say this: you must be and do before you can have. You must acquire a healthy self-image. You've got to like *you*. Positive thinking will not work for you if you can't see yourself as deserving the good things in life. It won't work if you don't think you deserve to be happy, if you don't think you deserve success, if you don't think you deserve a good husband or a good wife.

Moreover, if you're going to get to the top, you must develop a proper relationship with other people. We don't go through life by ourselves. You can climb the highest mountain, but only with the aid and cooperation of others.

If you go to an abandoned section of railroad track and watch the children walking down the rails, you'll see that they take a couple of steps, and off they'll come. Yet if you got them to hold hands across the rails, they could walk around the world together. I believe that if we get along with other people and work with them, we will get more out of life.

Next, you've got to have goals in life. Most people don't. Most people are wandering generalities, but you'll never make it that way. You must become a meaningful specific.

Can you imagine Sir Edmund Hillary, the first man to scale Mount Everest? Suppose that after he'd gotten up there, somebody had asked him, "Sir Edmund, how did you climb all the way to the top of the highest mountain in the world?" Would he have said, "Well, I was just out wandering around and . . ."?

You snicker, because it's utterly absurd that a man could climb the world's highest mountain without a plan. But it's even more ridiculous to think that we can develop our full potential unless we too have a very definite plan.

You've also got to have the right mental attitude. Most people have a good attitude when things are going well. When things are going badly, they have a bad attitude. You need to build an attitudinal foundation so that then when things go badly, you still have a good attitude, which means that soon things are going to be going well for you.

I'm going to have to introduce a word here: *work*. You can't be like this old boy down home. Somebody asked him how long he'd been working for his company, and he said, "Ever since they threatened to fire me." Some people quit looking for work as soon as they find a job. I was talking on the phone once with a man and asked, "How many people do you have working for you?" He said, "About half of them." That won't do it either.

For a number of years, I have gone around the country saying, "You've got to pay the price." As I did, I would assume a pained expression on my face and put a strain in my voice. But it's a bunch of baloney.

You don't pay the price for success. You don't pay the price for happiness. You don't pay the price for a good marriage. You don't pay the price to get the things that you really want out of life. You enjoy the price of success. You pay the price for failure.

Finally, if you're going to get the things you want out of life, you've got to live in a free enterprise system. I could not write this book in a communist country, because they do not believe in this system. But here, you can go where you want to go. You can do what you want to do. You can have what you want to have. You can be the way you want to be.

You are in luck, because you already have some of every quality that I've already discussed. You have some faith. You have some hope. You have some character. You have some loyalty. You have some integrity. You have some of a healthy self-image. There's something you like about yourself. You have some goals; they might be loosely defined, but you have some. Some of your attitude is right. You're willing to do some work. All we need to do is take what you've got and build on it to get what you really want.

I don't believe it takes much of a man or woman to be outstandingly successful. I don't believe they have to be six feet tall or have a college education. I don't believe these superficial qualities have anything really to do with success. It doesn't take much of a man or much of a woman to be successful, but it does take all of whatever you've got.

In the game of life, we do not have business failures: we have people failures. This book is going to talk about the people building business— the *you* building business.

I want to digress now to tell you a couple of stories which say a lot of the things that I really want to say. One is the story of the young couple on the road in a rural area. They were lost. They stopped at an old farm, and they said, "Sir, where will this road take us?" The old farmer said, "This road will take you anywhere in the world that you want to go, if you're moving in the right direction."

You can be on the right road and be heading in the wrong direction. You've got to be on the right road and heading in the right direction. If you're not, with this book, you've acquired the roadmap to get on the road.

The second story: A young business executive brought home an enormous amount of work to do that night. He had a little five-year-old son. I can tell you from experience that small children have an amazing capacity to ask an enormous number of questions at exactly the wrong time, so the little boy was asking question after question.

Finally his dad, seeing that he was not going to get his work done, devised a little plan. There was a map of the world in the newspaper. He tore it into pieces and told his son, "Son, put this map of the world back together." He figured that it would take the boy an hour or so; by then maybe he could have his work finished.

In about five minutes, the little boy came back and said, "Here it is, Daddy." The executive was amazed. He said, "Son, how did you put it together so fast?"

"It was easy, Daddy. On the other side of the map there was a picture of a man. As soon as I got the man right, the world was right."

When we're right individually, our world is right.

I also think of the story of the old Indian up in Oklahoma. A number of years ago, they discovered oil on his property. As he accumulated wealth, he started acquiring some of the material goods that go with it.

The old Indian had never had an automobile, so he bought a Cadillac, and it was a big one. In those days, they were touring cars; they used to have the spare tires on the back of the car. Instead of the usual two tires on the back, the old Indian added four additional tires. He bought himself a big, black Abraham Lincoln stovepipe hat, a tailcoat, a bow tie, a cigar— the whole works. He drove downtown every day in his automobile.

You could see the old Indian ride down the main street of this hot and dusty little Oklahoma town. He'd turn to the left, the right, and all the way around to speak to people, but he never ran into anybody, because directly in front of this big, beautiful automobile were two horses pulling it.

This is a true story. The old Indian had 100 horses ready, willing, and available, but he was using two on the outside because he had never learned how to insert the key and switch on the ignition.

This is the story of humankind. Scientists tell us that we today use approximately 2 percent of the ability that we have. We have 100 horses ready to go, and we end up using two. That's why Oliver Wendell Holmes said that the great tragedy in America is that the average man or woman goes to their grave with their music still in them. Those unplayed melodies are the most beautiful of all, but they never come forth.

Yes, I believe that the great tragedy in life is not to utilize the enormous abilities inside. To give you a challenge right now, do you realize that you're the only person in existence who will ever be able to use your ability? If you don't use it, it's going to be wasted; it's going to be gone forever.

I once heard a philosopher say, "You're where you are because that's exactly where you want to be."

"Man, that's right," I said. "That's truth if I've ever heard it." I went all over the country again saying, "You are where you are because that's exactly where you want to be," and the wise old owls out in the audience would nod and say, "That's exactly right."

Then one night I was in Birmingham, Alabama, on my way to Meridian, Mississippi. It was imperative that I be there the next morning. The roads were under repair, so I stopped at a service station to get directions. The attendant not only gave me directions but drew me a detailed map. He said, "Now, sir, if you will follow this map, I can assure you that you will be in Meridian in plenty of time without any difficulty."

I followed the map exactly as he had laid it out, but one hour later, I was forty-five miles further from Meridian, Mississippi, than I had been when I got the directions.

I was not there because that's where I wanted to be. No way. I was tired and sleepy. I wanted to be in bed. I was there because some well-intentioned dude had given me the wrong directions.

If you're not as far up the ladder of success, if you're not getting the things out of life that you really want, if you're not as happy and aren't accomplishing as much as you would like, maybe, just maybe, it has been because you have been given the wrong directions, and you might well have fallen victim to garbage dump thinking.

Now I'm going to tell you about garbage dump thinking, but before I do, I'm going to issue a warning and an apology. If you're one of these people who have gone through life making excuses, explaining why you can't do this and why you don't have that and why you don't contribute more—if you've been giving all of these excuses, I'm going to take all of them away from you forever. This book will pull the rug completely out from under you. Never again will you be able to complain that you lack the ability to accomplish what you want. If you're the kind of person who enjoys poor health, misery, and having people feeling sorry for you, then you'd better not read any further.

What is garbage dump thinking? Let me explain it this way: In a large Southern city, there's a magnificent new shopping center. For over 100 years, this shopping center was the site of the city dump. For over 100 years, they'd hauled garbage out and dumped it there. Finally, the local authorities saw that the city was growing in that direction, so they stopped dumping the garbage there and encouraged the local builders to take the excavated dirt from their construction sites and dump it instead. Over several years, they dumped tens of thousands of loads of good, clean, pure fill dirt on top of the old garbage dump.

One day, the builder looked at it and said, "The foundation is ready. Let's build a shopping center," and they did. So this shopping center is built on garbage.

I tell the story for a very simple reason: over a period of time, there might have been those who have been dumping garbage in your mind.

There might have been those who have built low ceilings there. There might have been those who have said, "You can't do it," or "You can only do so much." That is nothing but pure garbage, and I don't care how much of it has been dumped in your mind in the past. If I could, I would break out and sing "Happy Birthday." Today is in fact your happy birthday, because it's the first day of the rest of your life.

How many times have you thought, "Oh, if I could just start over"? This is it. This is your birthday. This is the chance for you to start over right now.

Let me offer another thought. Tons and tons of garbage might have been dumped in your mind for years—tens of thousands and even millions of statements of negativism. You cannot honestly expect to make one positive deposit on that big garbage dump and expect to overcome all of it.

We can begin by spreading a veneer to cover all of the garbage. This veneer will be fairly thin. At the first little setback, some of that old garbage underneath is going to break through, and you'll have stinkin' thinkin' again. You're going to have to put another veneer on, then another layer, and then another, until the day comes when you can completely bury all of that old garbage and build a magnificent future on it.

Are the things I'm saying facts or mere theory? Can we substantiate the validity of this philosophy?

Dr. William Glasser wrote a book entitled *Schools Without Failure*. In it, he tells about how they would take youngsters between eight and eleven years old who had never known anything but failure and put them in a new school. In the new school, they would no longer deal with the personalities, the problems, or the failures of the past. Instead they would take these kids and start dumping in the good, the clean, the pure, the powerful, and the positive stuff over and over: "You can, you can, you can." The results are absolutely dramatic.

There's a new school of psychology that does not lay you on the couch and say, "Now tell me what happened when you were five years old." Rather it takes people where they are and starts dealing with the present and burying the old problems of the past. With this approach, therapists look to the future. They build the good, the clean, the pure, the powerful, and the positive, and the results have been absolutely dramatic.

This puts man 2,000 years behind what God told us in his book. When he was on death row, the apostle Paul wrote, "Forgetting those things which are behind, and reaching forth unto those things which are before, I press toward the mark" (Philemon 3:13–14).

Muriel James and Dorothy Jongeward wrote a magnificent book entitled *Born to Win*. They point out that man was born to win, but over a period of time he has been conditioned to lose and develops what we call the loser's limp.

If you've ever watched a football game, you know what the loser's limp is. The offensive player gets behind the defensive player. He reaches up, grabs a pass, and streaks for the end zone. The defensive man quickly recovers and takes out in hot pursuit. When he gets about twenty yards from the end zone, though, the guy doing the chasing knows that he's not going to catch the guy with the ball; so does everybody in the stands. So what does the defensive man do? He pulls up limping. Everybody in the stands says, "No wonder the poor guy couldn't catch him. Why, shucks, he's crippled."

What is your loser's limp? Some people say, "I'm too old." Some say, "I'm too young." Some say, "I'm too fat." Some say, "I'm too skinny." Some say, "My skin color is wrong." Some blame the teacher or the preacher, and some blame the boss. Some say, "I was born under the wrong star."

In my travels from Perth, Australia, to Paris, France, I've met men and women from every race, creed, and color. I've seen them with every educational, social, and physical handicap known to man. Despite insurmountable odds, they never had a loser's limp, and as a result, they did an enormous amount of good.

I occasionally see someone stand up and say, "I'm a self-made man," but so far I've never seen someone stand up and say, "I'm a self-made failure." Instead, they blame everybody else. Some blame all of society. But I want you to notice one thing. When you've got one finger, your forefinger, pointed away, you've got three fingers pointed right back at you. If you really want to make certain of finding a helping hand, just look down at the end of your sleeve, and there that hand is going to be.

Some people say, "I'm just not a natural born" doctor or lawyer or salesman or teacher or whatever it is. I don't know what you've observed, but I've seen where women have given birth to boys. I've seen where they've given birth to girls. But I've never seen where a woman has given birth to a doctor, a lawyer, or a salesman. Yet all of these people die, so obviously somewhere between birth and death, by choice and by training, they become what they want to become.

People with loser's limps are prisoners of hope. They hope that someday they're going to be walking down Main Street, see a box, and give it a kick, and out of it will come their own personal fortune in gems or jewels. They say, "I don't believe in luck, but just maybe I might hit the jackpot on this lottery, and then I'll live happily ever after." There's not much consistency there.

Some people say, "Oh, if I could just be a little smarter." Did you ever ask God to make you smarter? The New Testament says, "If any of you lack wisdom, let him ask of God, that giveth to all men liberally. . . . But let him ask in faith, nothing withholding" (James 1:5–6). But how do most people pray? "Lord, make me smarter. Of course, I know you won't." That's not exactly what I call a prayer.

A number of years ago, an old recluse lived in the city of Venice. It was said of this old man that he could answer any question that anybody might ask of him. One day, two small boys determined to fool the old man. They caught a little bird, and they approached him. One of the boys held the little bird in his hand and asked, "Old man, is this bird alive or is he dead?"

Without changing expression, the old man said, "Son, if I say to you that that bird is alive, you will simply close your hands and crush him, and he'll be dead. If I say to you that this little bird is dead, you'll simply open your hands, and he will fly away, because in your hands you hold the power of life or death."

In your hands, you hold the seeds of failure or the seeds of success. They're capable hands, but they're *your* hands, and your decision will determine how successful, happy, and fulfilled you will be.

If you just read my message and do nothing about it, it's done nobody any good. The man who won't read is no better off than the man who can't read. The person who won't act on success principles is no better off than the one who has never heard those principles. If we're going to get anything in life, we've got to get started in order to get it.

I was raised in a little town down in Mississippi. We lived next door to some rich folks. I know they were rich for two reasons: number one, they had a cook; number two, the cook had something to cook. During the Depression, that was a sure sign of wealth.

Now don't misunderstand. We had plenty to eat at my house. I know we had plenty because if I ever passed my plate for seconds, they'd always tell me, "No, you've had plenty."

I was over at the rich folks' house for lunch one day, as I tried to be most every day. They brought the biscuits out, and the biscuits were flat. I said, "What in the world happened to your biscuits?"

The cook reared back, gave a big old tummy laugh, and said, "I'll tell you about those biscuits. They squatted to rise. They just got cooked in the squat."

The people who wait until everything is just right before doing anything are the ones that get cooked in the squat. We see people like that all the time. They're going to do something just as soon as John gets on the day shift and things are a little more normal, or just as soon as they finish spring housecleaning, or just as soon as the kids go back to school.

Imagine where you would be if before a big meeting, you called the chief of police and said, "Chief, I've got a meeting to go to. But before I leave, tell me, chief, are all the lights on green? If they're on green, I'm going to go. But if they're not on green, I'm not going to go." The chief would have thought he was talking to some kind of nut, and he would have been right. Those who wait until everything is just right before they do anything are always going to end up cooked in the squat.

Years ago in New York City, a man was selling balloons. When business slowed down, he would release one. As it rose into the air, the crowd would gather, and his business would be brisk for a few minutes. He released a red one, then a white one, and then a yellow one. Presently, a little black boy walked up to him, tugged on his sleeves, and said, "Mister, if you released the black balloon, would it go up?"

The man looked down at the little boy and, with a wisdom and compassion that belied his profession, said, "Son, it's what's inside of the balloon that makes it go up."

It's what's inside of us—in our hearts—that make us go up. If we've got that right, we can acquire the other characteristics.

Regardless of whether you're in Decision Valley or on Hesitation Hill, or even if your career or personal life are already in high gear, let me urge you to fasten your seat belt, because you are on a trip to the top. It's an exciting trip, with more suspense than an Alfred Hitchcock thriller. It has more action than a John Wayne Western, more drama than a Shakespearean play, and more fun than a three-ring circus. It's immersed in love, it's filled with laughter, and it offers more true rewards than King Solomon's mines.

In short, this book is the owner's manual for your future. But if you're going to get the things in life you want, you've got to start.

2

The Power of Self-Image

This chapter has five purposes:

1. To demonstrate the importance of a healthy self-image.
2. To identify the causes of a poor self-image.
3. To reveal the manifestations of a poor self-image.
4. To give you some methods for improving your self-image.
5. To encourage you to choose and remain on the road to a healthy self-image.

Those are our objectives, and I'm confident that as you go through this chapter, you're going to see some changes take place in yourself even before you finish it.

God said to build a better world, and I said, "How? The world is such a cold, dark place and so complicated now. And I'm so young and useless; there's nothing I can do." But God in all his wisdom said, "Just build a better you."

We've got to have a healthy self-image before we can accomplish anything. We will perform exactly the way we see ourselves.

I'd like to begin by telling you about three thieves. The first is a man named Emanuel Ninger. Let me take you back to the year 1887. The scene is a small neighborhood grocery store. A gentleman is buying some turnip greens from the clerk. He hands her a $20 bill, and as she starts to put it in the cash drawer, she notices that the ink is coming off on her hands. She looks at it in shock and astonishment, because she has known Emanuel Ninger for a long period of time. He's a neighbor. He's a friend. He's traded there for years. She is certain that Emanuel Ninger would never give her a counterfeit $20 bill, so she gives him the change.

But then the clerk got to thinking. Twenty dollars was an awful lot of money in 1887, so she called the police. Two policemen came out. One looked at it and said, "Man, I wish I had a thousand of them." The other one said, "If it's genuine, why is the ink coming off?"

Curiosity combined with the responsibility demanded that they get a warrant to search the house of Emanuel Ninger. They went through it, and up in the attic, they found the facilities for reproducing $20 bills. The facilities were fairly simple: they consisted of an easel, some brushes, and some paint. There in front of them was a $20 bill in the very act of being counterfeited.

Emanuel Ninger counterfeited his $20 bills by painting them. He was a master artist, so skillful that if the clerk had not had wet hands, he might never have been discovered. Oh, he was a marvelous artist.

While they were in the attic, the police made another discovery. They discovered three portraits that Emanuel Ninger had painted. Those portraits sold at auction for a little over $16,000—more than $5,000 for each one. It took Emanuel Ninger approximately the same length of time to paint a $20 bill as it did to paint a portrait that sold for over $5,000.

Emanuel Ninger was quite a thief. But, of course, the person he was stealing the most from was obviously Emanuel Ninger. You see, he could have been successful. He could have made enormous sums of money while making a contribution to society, but he didn't understand the basic principle that you can get everything you want if you'll help enough other people get what they want. He tried to take a shortcut, and it never works.

I'm going to bring you forward a little bit, to Boston in the Roaring Twenties. The second thief I'd like to share with you is Arthur Barry. Arthur

Barry was a jewel thief, and a good one. He was so good that for years he eluded the police.

Arthur Barry was also a very discriminating man. He would not steal from just anybody. Oh, no, not Arthur Barry. He was very selective in the people that he stole from. Not only must they have money, but they must be in the top echelons of society. It became somewhat of a status symbol to have been called on by Arthur Barry.

The police did not share the enthusiasm of these socialites.

One night they caught him and shot him three times. As he lay there, bullets in his body, splinters of glass in his eyes, suffering excruciating pain, he made a not too surprising statement: "I ain't going to do this anymore."

Amazingly, Arthur Barry made good his escape. For the next three years he lived outside of the law. No one could find out where he was. Then one day a jealous woman turned him in, and he went out to the federal penitentiary, where he served something like seventeen years. When he got out of prison, he settled in a small New England community, and he kept his word. He did not go back to being a thief.

Arthur Barry became a model citizen. He became so respected that his community elected him commander of a local veteran's organization. But then, as it inevitably will, word leaked out, and reporters gathered from all over the country. They had found Arthur Barry, and they wanted to interview this man. They fired questions at him. Finally, one young reporter got at the crux of the matter, asking, "Mr. Barry, in your career as a jewel thief, you stole from an awful lot of people. But let me ask you: do you recall in your years as a thief the one from whom you stole the most?"

Without a moment's hesitation, Arthur Barry said, "That's easy. The man from whom I stole the most was Arthur Barry. You see, I spent two thirds of my adult life behind prison bars. As a free man, as a contributing member of society, I could have become a successful businessman, a baron on Wall Street. But I tried to take the shortcuts. I tried to get something for nothing, and I ended up stealing from Arthur Barry."

Many people are like Arthur Barry: they go through life trying to take the shortcuts and end up stealing from themselves.

The third thief I would like to introduce you to is *you*. I believe that any man, woman, boy, or girl who does not utilize the enormous potential that they have inside of themselves is a thief.

How do we quit stealing from ourselves? I want to challenge you with an enormous, awesome responsibility: of all of the people on the face of this earth, you are the only one who can use your ability.

Let's pretend that your telephone rings tomorrow morning, and the voice at the other end is that of an old and respected friend. You know that this individual calling you is very sincere and conscientious about everything he says.

This friend says to you, "John, don't get uptight. I haven't called to ask any favors. I just wanted to call you—and I should have called you years ago to tell you this—to tell you, John, that I think you're one of the nicest guys who has ever drawn a breath of air. You're an asset to this community. You're a credit to your profession. You're the kind of guy that I like to be with and around, because every time I'm with you I'm always excited, I'm motivated, I'm enthused, I'm turned on. John, if I could see you five minutes a day, I could turn this world upside down, because you're such a tremendous individual. That's all I wanted to say, and I look forward to seeing you soon." And he hangs up.

This is an old and respected friend. You know he's deadly sincere in everything that he's saying to you. Let me ask you: what kind of a day would you have? If you were baking a cake, would you bake a better cake? If you were a mother, would you be a better mother? If you were a teacher, would you be a better teacher? If you were a housewife, would you be a better housewife? If you were a doctor, would you be a better doctor? If you were a student, would you make better grades? Would you be better doing everything in life that you do?

Here's another question: how much more would you know about baking a cake, teaching, keeping house, being a mother, being a doctor, or anything else? I think the answer is completely obvious: you would not know any more. Yet there is absolutely no doubt that you would be better at what you do, because the image that you have of yourself has now undergone a dramatic change: "I'm an asset to my community. I'm a credit to my profession. That old boy said so, and he is one smart cookie."

One way to build a healthy self-image is by helping someone else. Since that kind of praise would make you feel so good, why don't you give it to someone else? Call someone and say some nice things to them: "You are an asset. You are a nice fellow. You are a nice girl. You inspire a lot of people."

Obviously, they will be terribly excited and turned on. But guess who will be even more enthusiastic? That's right. You will stand tall in your own eyes, because, again, you can get everything in life that you want if you'll just help enough other people get what they want.

Dr. David McClelland at Harvard University did a twenty-five-year study and found that motivation is more important for success than many of the other factors that people have stressed in times past. He found that if you're going to change your performance, you must change the way you see yourself and your circumstances.

That is exactly what this book is all about—to change the way you see yourself and your circumstances.

The story of Victor Serebriakoff emphasizes what I want to say. When he was fifteen, his teacher said to him, "Victor, you're a dunce. You're never going to pass. You're never going to be able to graduate from school. Why don't you drop out? Why don't you get a job? Learn a trade. When you're an adult, you will at least be able to support yourself."

Here's an authority saying, "Victor, you're stupid." And in effect Victor said, "Yes, ma'am," or "Yes, sir." He dropped out of school, and for the next sixteen years, he became an itinerant, traveling all over the country and doing 101 different things.

When Victor was thirty years old, they did a psychological evaluation on him and made an astonishing discovery. They discovered that he had an IQ of 161. He was a genius.

For all those years, Victor Serebriakoff had been getting up every morning and shaving a dunce, dressing a dunce, going to work as a dunce, performing as a dunce, and receiving a dunce's paycheck.

All of a sudden, somebody comes along and says, "Victor, you're not a dunce; you're a genius." Now Victor Serebriakoff, without learning one fact, except the most important one of them all—that he's not a dunce—gets up as a genius, shaves a genius, dresses a genius, and goes to work as a genius, and he's been getting a genius's paycheck for years. He's written several books, has a number of patents to his credit, and is an enormously successful businessman. He was elected as the international chairman of Mensa, the oldest and largest high-IQ society in the world. You've got to have an IQ of 132 just to get into Mensa.

What happened to Victor Serebriakoff? Not a thing, except that he learned the truth about himself—that there was enormous potential inside of him.

You were designed for accomplishment, engineered for success, and endowed with the seeds of greatness. But you've got to acknowledge that fact, because you're going to perform exactly as you see yourself.

Mildred Newman and Bernard Berkowitz wrote a book entitled *How to Be Your Own Best Friend*, in which they ask a penetrating question: if we cannot love ourselves, where will we draw our love for anyone else? I'm not talking about a superinflated ego, because conceit is a weird disease that makes everybody sick except the one that's got it.

In *Born to Win*, Muriel James and Dorothy Jongeward argue that humans were born to win but over a period of time have been conditioned to lose. Again, you cannot perform in a manner that is inconsistent with the way you see yourself. And of all the gifts the Creator gives us, surely the gift of choosing the way that we wish to be is one of the greatest of them all.

Before Michelangelo ever struck the first blow on his statue of the mighty Moses, he looked at that block of granite and saw Moses in his entirety residing in the granite. The mind completes the picture that you put in it. Whether it's good, bad, or indifferent, winning or losing, the mind goes to work to complete the image that is there.

I'm sure you've heard this analogy: I could take a twelve-inch plank and stretch it across the floor, and I could call on anyone to walk it. Everybody would say, "Ziglar, that's ridiculous. Anybody can walk a plank that's twelve inches wide." But if we were to take the plank and put it between two twenty-story buildings, everybody would say, "Ziglar, that's ridiculous. I would fall and break my silly neck." In many cases you would, because the moment you stepped on the plank, the fear of falling would come into your mind, and you'd say, "I'm afraid I'm going to fall." The mind completes the picture that you put in it.

Job tells us in the Bible: "The thing which I greatly feared is come upon me" (Job 3:25). If you play golf, you've been out on the course with somebody who steps up to the tee and dribbles the ball in the lake. What do they say as they turn back? "I knew I was going to do that."

The mind completes the picture that we put into it, and for many people, a poor self-image is the net result. That's one reason people never reach beyond their ceilings. They never strive to get a better job, because they cannot see themselves as deserving a magnificent automobile, a beautiful home, a fine income, or a vacation in Hawaii. Because they cannot see themselves as deserving these things, they never make the effort to acquire them. They resign from life without ever giving it a chance to do the things for them that it would if they saw themselves properly.

I've seen this happen in every World Series that I've ever had the privilege of watching: the batter will step up, and he'll let that third strike go right past him. He's going to be called out without ever taking the bat off his shoulders. Having the chance to get a hit, even a home run, or advance a man on a base, he never takes the bat off his shoulders. The net result is, nothing happens.

Even more disappointing is the individual who never gets into the game of life, who never takes the bat off their shoulders, who never gets involved, because they never see themselves as capable or deserving of accomplishment. That's partly why Dr. Maxwell Maltz contended in one of his books that the sole purpose of psychotherapy—in any form—is to change the image of the patient. Dr. Joyce Brothers also observed that what we select as an income, what we select as a job, the friends and habits we select— every feature of our lives—is controlled by the way we see ourselves.

Again, it's not the ability that we have that is important, but rather it's the way we see ourselves. Many surveys have been done on movie stars. Without exception, the Hollywood beauties, the glamour girls, the models are all continually saying, "If I could just change this feature . . ." Regardless of how beautiful they are, they never quite see themselves as being really attractive.

Once I was driving out of Raleigh, North Carolina; this was in the days when it was reasonably safe to pick up a hitchhiker. Because of the enormous amount of hitchhiking experience I'd had in my youth, I picked a hitchhiker up.

When the man sat down, I realized immediately that I'd made a mistake, because he was drinking a little and talking a mile a minute.

I wanted to make friends with the guy, because I didn't know what the result might be otherwise. I said, "How are you doing?"

"Fine. Just got out of prison."

"When?"

"About three hours ago."

I really wanted to keep the conversation light from then on in. I asked, "What were you in for?"

"Bootlegging."

"How long were you in for?"

"A couple of years." He never did give me an exact figure.

I said, "Did you learn anything while you were in there?"

"What do you mean?"

"Did you learn anything? Did you acquire new skills? Any job training? Any expertise that will enable you to make a living doing anything other than being a bootlegger?"

"Yeah," he said, "I did learn something. I learned the names of every county in every state in the United States and every parish in the State of Louisiana."

"Man, you've got to be kidding."

"Just try me on one. Name a state that you're familiar with, and see if I can't name the counties."

"I spent sixteen years in South Carolina; what about South Carolina?"

He started, "Abbeville, Anderson . . . " He went right down the list and, without pause or hesitation, named every county in the State of South Carolina. He said, "Give me another one."

"No," I said, "you've got me convinced."

Here's the thing that is so astonishing. Here was a man who very obviously had a very limited education. You listened to him, and you were aware that it could not have been more than the second, third, or fourth grade at the most. But he had assigned his mind a task, and it learned every county in every state, and I'm convinced that he knew them all.

Why the man selected this inconsequential information to acquire, I don't know. But it emphasizes a point: he had the mental ability, but he saw himself as a bootlegger. He saw himself only as acquiring nonsensical information, and he did not utilize his enormous mind power.

Many people confuse education with intelligence. They say, "I only finished the third grade," or "I only finished the fifth grade," or "I only finished the eighth grade." Let me emphasize a point: the three most brilliant, successful people I've ever met in my life finished the third, the fifth, and the eighth grades respectively.

It's not how much money you make that determines your success. Rather it's the amount of success you enjoy relative to the ability that you have. One man could make $10,000 a year and be enormously successful. Another could make $50,000 a year and be unsuccessful, according to the amount of ability he has related to the ability he uses.

Almost without exception, in the game of life you measure a person's contribution by the amount of money he earns. Notice that I said, *"almost* without exception." If we're in the sales world, for example, if we're selling a legitimate product at a fair profit and earn $50,000 a year, it's because we're helping a lot of people solve the problems with the product we're selling.

The exceptions are easy to identify. Many times, as you know, there are rural schoolteachers or ministers who for one reason or another have been called to serve in that particular community. Their reward comes directly from the amount of service they are rendering. But in ninety-nine cases out of 100, you can say that the person who is rendering large amounts of service is the person who is going to be earning large sums of money.

Let's look at the causes of a poor self-image, because before we can get at solving the problem, we have to find out what caused it to begin with.

I'm persuaded beyond any reasonable doubt that unfortunately, in the greatest land on the face of this earth, we are living in an essentially negative society. The overweight person sits down at the table and says, "Everything I eat turns to fat." A little boy comes home from school and says, "Dad, I'm afraid I failed the arithmetic test." His dad says, "Don't sweat it, son. I never could learn the stuff either." A housewife looks at her house, and it's a wreck. She says, "I'll never get this mess cleaned up." She's like the lady whose home was so bad that *Good Housekeeping* canceled her subscription.

Often a mother will send her child off to school saying, "Now don't get run over." Negative, negative, negative. Or we start out on a picnic, and there's a little sprinkling. We say, "I knew it would. It always does. Every time we plan something, this is exactly what happens." Even the weatherman gets in on this act. He comes on the television and says, "We have a 40 percent chance of rain." Why doesn't the dirty dog tell us we have a 60 percent chance of sunshine?

Some people find fault as if there's a reward for it. Because they do, we end up with a poor self-image. Many of the problems start in childhood. A child drops something, and the parent will say, "You're always dropping things." A little boy starts out to go to school. His shirttail hangs out, and the parent says, "You never look nice." This constant negative input has a devastating effect as it's played in the mind over and over.

I don't know why we can't understand that there's a vast amount of difference between doing something bad and being bad. Kids all do bad things. I've never seen one that didn't—even my own four. But they're not bad kids just because they did a bad thing. We need to keep things in perspective.

Many times parents make the mistake of bragging about the physical appearance of another child. This is devastating to your own child. Never, never, never brag about the physical appearance of another child in the presence of your own. Never say, "My, what a pretty little girl. My, what a handsome little boy," because your children will get the idea that you regard physical attractiveness as a desirable characteristic. They will negate themselves, saying, "I'm not as pretty as she is," or "I'm not as handsome as he is."

What should you as a parent say about another child? You take the positive approach as it relates both to that child and to your own. Simply say, "My, doesn't he have beautiful manners?" or "Isn't this a thoughtful girl? Isn't she enthusiastic?" or "Isn't he considerate?" Praise the qualities in the other child that you want to develop in your own.

The same thing applies in marital relationships. The smart man will never say, "That sure is a pretty girl," in the presence of his wife, because she will automatically think, "He thinks she is prettier than I am." If your wife already has a poor self-image, you've just sown the seeds for problems.

To my mind, there's absolutely no doubt that the greatest damage that the white man has ever done to the black man has to do with the effect we have had on his self-image.

I'm going to date myself. The famed child actress Shirley Temple and I are about the same age. When I was a little fellow, I would go to the movies and see Little Miss Lollipop singing and dancing.

But here is a scene whose real meaning I did not see until much later. Little Shirley Temple, five years old, is having a birthday party. A black girl of about fourteen or fifteen comes to the party, along with three or four of her little buddies, who are about five or six. The black girl has brought Miss Shirley a present. Miss Shirley says, "Oh, thank you. Won't you have some birthday cake? We've got some left." The fourteen-year-old black girl starts to cry because the five-year-old white girl is offering her some leftover birthday cake.

I don't think I have to elaborate on what this does to the self-image of black people. Recent decades have been the most progressive of all eras in improving black self-esteem. The progress will be still more rapid when blacks and whites understand that the pigment in the skin has absolutely nothing to do with the ability in the body or the way Almighty God looks at each one of us as individuals.

Jesse Owens, the great black Olympic champion, said that black is not beautiful; white is not beautiful. He said, "Those are skin colors. If it's only skin deep, friend, that's not beautiful." I couldn't agree more.

Another thing that causes a poor self-image is confusing failure in a project with failure in life. We might flunk a history test, but that doesn't make us a failure in life. We might not make the first team, but that does not make a failure in life. There are certain things that on occasion we're not capable of doing. Just because we've failed at one item does not mean we're failures as people.

I frequently use this idea when I'm in sales training: 90 percent of the national sales champions, regardless of what company they represent, miss more sales in a given year than any other salesperson with the company. They've failed more times than anybody else, but they kept making the calls and did not confuse a failure on a call with failure in life.

People sometimes develop a poor self-image because they have a lousy memory. They keep saying, "I can't remember this; I can't remember that. I don't have a good memory. Therefore I'm a nothing."

Listen: a good memory has no more to do with a great mind than the dictionary has to do with a great piece of literature. If this will give you some comfort, let me throw this one in: it is far better not to have the capacity to remember everything than it is not to have the ability to forget some of the things that happen in the game of life.

Now that I've said that, though, let me urge you to buy *The Memory Book*, by Harry Lorayne and Jerry Lucas, which contends that there is no such thing as a good memory or a bad memory. It's a matter of either a trained memory or an untrained memory.

People may develop a poor self-image because they make the mistake of comparing experience. They say, "I can't do this, and that fellow can; therefore, I'm not as capable as he is."

Let's shoot that down in a big hurry. Millions of Australians can do something that few Americans can do. They can drive down the left-hand side of the highway—safely. Does that mean they're smarter than you? No, it means they've had a different experience.

Hundreds of millions of Chinese children can do something that most of us can't. They can speak Chinese. That's exactly right. Now does that make them smarter than we are? I don't think so. It does mean that they've had a different experience.

Let me tell you about a humbling experience that I had. I got stuck in the alley in back of my house. I don't know why I had to feel that I had to drive down it that night. I didn't ordinarily, and there had been a heavy rain.

I got stuck right in back of my house. I wrestled with the car for a few minutes and saw that it wasn't coming out. I said, "Nobody is going to be as big an idiot as I was. They surely won't come down this alley tonight. I'll wait till tomorrow morning. Maybe it'll dry a little bit, and I can drive the car out."

I got up the next morning, went out, got in, and started the car, and nothing happened. I got some boards and bricks and sand, and I wrestled with that thing for about twenty minutes. I must have burned 5,000 miles in wear off those tires.

Finally, I called the wrecker. The man came out, and I don't believe he got beyond the second day of the first grade of school. He walked around the car for a minute or two and said, "Let me see your key."

I said, "What for?"

"I think I can drive it out."

"Man, ain't no way. I wrestled with this thing for thirty minutes. It cannot be done."

"Well," he said, "I think I can."

I gave him the key. I was perfectly willing to accept his apology very graciously a few minutes later.

The wrecker got in, inserted the key, cranked the engine, turned the wheel slightly, and rocked it twice. It must have taken him ten seconds to drive that car right out of the hole that I'd wrestled with for so long.

When he came out, I said, "I just don't understand that. I wrestled with that thing thirty minutes."

He just grinned and said, "To tell you the truth, I was raised over in East Texas. I've been driving out of gully washers bigger than that since I was ten years old."

All he was saying to me was, "My friend, I have had a different experience than yours."

When we look at what somebody else is doing, let's remember that they've had a different experience. They decided by choice that that's what they wanted to do, and you have made your decision as to what you want to do.

A lot of people develop a negative self-image because they make the mistake of comparing their worst features to somebody else's best features.

To illustrate the point, there was a thirty-eight-year-old scrubwoman. Bless her heart, she'd been born ugly, and then somebody scared her. She bought a book, *The Magic of Believing*. She read the book, believed it, and got motivated, but she didn't get pretty.

This woman didn't try to compete with the glamour girls of Hollywood, but she started taking inventory of the assets that she did have. She said, "When I was in school, I used to make people laugh. I think that's what I'll do."

This woman, Phyllis Diller, started making people laugh so much that she earned millions of dollars. She did not let what she did not have keep her from using what she did have. That's terribly important for all of us to remember.

Jimmy Durante and Humphrey Bogart were not exactly poster material, but they took what they had and used it and didn't worry about what they didn't have. Durante obviously took the lemon and made lemonade out of it.

Many people say, "If I had somebody else's ability, what wouldn't I do?" The answer: you can't do a cotton-picking thing with somebody else's ability if you are not using your own. What makes you think you can use somebody else's abilities if you're not using the ones you have? Even if you got your wish, six weeks later, you'd be saying, "What I really wanted was the one right over there."

You surely remember the parable of the talents in the Bible. One servant had one talent, one had two, and one had five. Their master went away to a far country, and he came back. He went to the servant who had five and said, "How'd you do?"

The fella said, "Lord, I really did good. I took the five and put them to work. Now I've got ten."

The master said, "That's good," went to the servant that had two talents, and said, "How did you do?"

"Lord, I really did good. I took the two and put them to work. Now I've got four."

The Lord said, "That's really good." He went to the servant who had one talent and said, "How'd you do?"

The servant said, "Lord, you really didn't do me right. That dude over there, you gave him two. And that fella, you gave five. And poor little me, all you did, Lord, was just give me one. I knew that you were a hard and cruel master. I knew that you reaped where you had not sown, so I took the talent and buried it." Hear the crybabies of life saying, "I don't have more, so I'm not going to use what I've got."

The master looked at this man and addressed him with the hardest words that you'll ever find in the New Testament: "You wicked and slothful servant! Because you have not used the one talent I gave you, I'm going to take it away from you and give it to the servant who has ten" (Matthew 25:14–28).

God says, "For unto every one that hath shall be given, and he shall have abundance: but from him that hath not shall be taken away even that which he hath" (Matthew 25:28), meaning simply that if we don't take what we've got and use it, we're going to lose it. But if we do take what we've got and use it, the Lord will increase what we already have.

What are some of the manifestations of a poor self-image? How can you tell? How can you identify it if you've got one? How can you tell if your friends have got one?

There are a number of manifestations of a poor self-image. One is jealousy. A woman says, "I love my man so much I don't ever want him out of my sight." Baloney. What she's really saying is, "I don't like myself; therefore, I cannot believe that he could love me above all other women on the face of this earth."

Obviously the same thing happens with men. This jealousy is the result of a poor self-image. These people don't love themselves, so they can't imagine anybody else loving them above all other people.

Another manifestation is gossip. Gossips are always talking about other people. They keep unfounded rumors alive. They haven't learned that when you're throwing dirt, you're not doing a thing in the world but losing ground.

Another manifestation: people who can't even stand constructive criticism from someone else. If the boss says something constructive, they misunderstand it and take it personally, because they don't like themselves and don't think the other person likes them.

People with a poor self-image cannot stand it if somebody laughs at them. It tears them to pieces.

Let me emphasize here that I think one of the healthiest things in the world is a sense of humor. You will notice all the way through this book that humor prevails. But you'll also notice that it's never any sick kind of humor, putting down a person's race, religion, color, or sex. It is a building kind of a humor rather than the kind that would hurt anyone.

The person with a poor self-image cannot stand to be alone. You'll often see him walking down the street, carrying a radio and snapping his fingers. These people frequently adopt an "I don't care" attitude, because they can't see themselves as winning. On many occasions, they deliberately dress unattractively and forgo personal hygiene. I've never been able to understand how anybody could feel that being dirty proves anything other than that they have not been close to a bar of soap. Others with a poor self-image use profane language, become obese, abandon morality, or turn to drugs.

A poor self-image is also revealed in self-sabotaging behavior. An athlete may have spent four years getting ready for the Olympics; then, the day before the competition, he pulls a muscle or strains a ligament or has an injury that keeps him from competing. He cannot see himself as deserving this particular award, so he does something to avoid it.

In another instance, a student trying to get into a school will stay up at night and get drunk the night before an important test. He's been saying for years that he wants to get into the college of his choice. He has the chance but deliberately does something that lessens his chances of getting there.

Men on probation tell me they do exactly the same thing. They deliberately commit some senseless crime—a misdemeanor, in most cases—that violates their parole. They're thrown back into jail. The net result is over an 80 percent rate of recidivism in prisons.

If you're in sales, a poor self-image will keep you from making a call, closing a sale, or trying to share a business opportunity. Every time you offer to sell somebody something, a certain risk is involved. When you take this risk, the person slams the door in your face. You don't like you, so you think they don't like you.

As a result, a salesperson with a poor self-image decides to drink a cup of coffee and think about what to do. While they're drinking the first cup, they decide they deserve the second. Then they remember, "I've got to get organized. That's my problem." Even though it's only Tuesday afternoon, they decide to take care of all the details so they can get a fresh start next Monday morning. This is nothing more than the result of a poor self-image.

When a salesperson with a healthy self-image has the door slammed in their face, they understand that they've got a problem: someone has slammed the door in their face. They go next door to find somebody who does not have that problem.

Another form of self-sabotage is to deliberately provoke an argument with a spouse right before one is going in for an important interview or promotion. The individual provokes the argument, so they're not at their best; then they blame the spouse for their failure to get the job.

It's difficult for a person with a poor self-image to move into administration or management. When they do, they frequently step out of character. They become good old Joe and say to everybody, "Nothing has changed." Or they become the opposite: arrogant and conceited. "I know it all, and I'm going to show everybody a thing or two." Their relationship with management is sometimes bad. They become overanxious to please; they eat too much humble pie; they become servile. Their minds are paralyzed by fear. They're so afraid they're going to make a mistake that they never do anything: they become managers by crisis.

On the other side of the ledger, people with a healthy self-image move into management with a cautious confidence that shows they are qualified to do the job. They're short on promises but long on fulfillment. They understand the difference between serving and being servile (and there is a great deal of difference). They neither seek nor avoid confrontations and meet decision making head on. They understand that they have been promoted because management had confidence in their ability to do the job or grow into it.

These individuals know where to draw the line between confidence and arrogance. More importantly, they can be firm on principle but flexible on method. They draw the line between being friendly and being familiar.

They don't get all shook up when they make a wrong decision, because they know that in most cases the worst decision is no decision. They can act decisively, and they don't feel threatened when they are mistaken or challenged or when they have to ask for help.

In the family, a poor self-image is manifested in people who will not discipline their children. Many times, I have had a young father or mother say to me, "I love my child too much to spank him," or "It hurts me worse than it does them." They're really saying, "I'm afraid that if I discipline my child, the child is going to withhold their love from me. I'm so insecure in myself that I am not going to do that."

The child's respect for authority is lost at home, then it's lost further in school. When they get out in life to compete, they have no respect for any authority anywhere. I believe fervently that we must return to the principle of teaching courteous discipline to our children.

Dr. Forest Tennant at UCLA is an expert on substance abuse and has done perhaps the most comprehensive study on the drug problem. He studied the problem with our GIs in Germany. He discovered that among all the thousands of men he studied, only two factors served as a deterrent to drug use: (1) if the individual had been taken to church—I said *taken*, not *sent*—fifty or more times before the age of fifteen; and (2) if he had been regularly but moderately spanked. I was quoted once in a newspaper: "Ziglar says, 'Spank him and take him to church if you don't want him to use drugs,'" and that's pretty accurate. That's exactly what I did say. I did, however, say, spank *moderately.*

I firmly believe that discipline is important. I'll never forget when my oldest daughter was a junior in high school. She came to me one evening and said, "Dad, I want to go to such-and-such a place."

I said, "Tell me about it." She told me, and I said, "Absolutely not."

She clouded up as if she was going to rain, and she said, "How come? Everybody else is going."

"The fact that everybody else is going has absolutely no bearing on whether you go or not."

"Why?"

"Because I love you too much to let you go to a place of that nature with those people. You belong neither in that place nor with those people."

My daughter stood there for ten or fifteen seconds. Her lips quivered. She jumped up, grabbed me around the neck, gave me the biggest kiss any daddy ever got, and said, "Thank you, Daddy. I didn't want to go anyhow." Many times our kids will try us. The greatest thing we can do is to let them know that we love them.

Let's look at some manifestations of a poor self-image in other areas of life. A student with a poor self-image will sometimes deserve a better grade and yet never ask the teacher why.

Many times, a guy with a poor self-image won't ask a pretty girl for a date because he doesn't think he deserves it. That's one reason we see some of the ugliest men marry the most beautiful girls: even though they might not be physically handsome, they've got a good self-image.

The person with the poor self-image won't assert himself and seek a raise even when he knows he deserves it. The company doesn't give it to him automatically, and he becomes resentful. His production goes down, and he ends up losing his job when he would have gotten the raise if he had simply said, "I'm worth more money."

A poor self-image is revealed in some amazing ways. Good old Joe, everybody's friend, in reality has a poor self-image. He gives up his place at the front of the line, letting people crowd in front of him. He never talks back to anybody. He becomes a doormat because he wants to be popular with everybody.

Now don't misunderstand. If you do those things because you have so much confidence that it doesn't bother you, that's one thing. Otherwise, it's another story.

Joe's problem is a common one, and it's no respecter of age, sex, education, size, or skin color. He thinks, "I must be a nice guy and never offend anyone." As a youngster, he smokes cigarettes he doesn't want. He lights the joint or takes the drink he doesn't like. He laughs at dirty jokes that offend him. He joins the gang he secretly dislikes and goes along with conduct and participates in a dress code that he secretly abhors. It's all because he has never accepted himself, and he is terribly concerned that if he asserts himself and crosses someone else, he will not have any friends.

Sad Joe and his female counterpart are inclined to marry their first serious romantic interest. The fear of not being accepted by anyone else frequently leads them to foolish and impetuous action, including early marriage.

When one of my daughters was a senior in high school, she was talking about somebody she wanted to go with. I didn't approve of it, and she said, "Daddy, all of the good boys are soon going to be gone."

I said, "Baby, somehow or another, I think there's going to be a supply of boys from here on in, and I don't believe I'd worry about it." Later, she acknowledged that there is a pretty good supply of boys all over the place.

As an adult, this person tends to tell people only what he thinks they want to hear. He'd never send an overcooked steak back to the kitchen. He'd never complain if the doctor kept him sitting in the office for an hour.

Every area of life and every occupation is affected by poor self-image. If you think you fit into the group with a poor self-image, let me urge you not to fume or fret, because I'm going to give you some step-by-step procedures to correct your poor self-image and to make a good one better. You are now ready to start stepping up the stairs to success, and you're going to discover you'll move up the stairs faster after you get out of the crowd at the bottom. And that's exactly what you're going to be doing.

3

How to Build a
Healthy Self-Image

I've discussed the importance of a healthy self-image as well as the manifestations of a poor one. How do you build a healthy self-image?

Any company, if it were to go out of business, would first conduct an inventory. It would take stock of its assets and set a fair market value for them. Let's hold a going out of business sale for you. Let's say that you've decided to retire from life. You want to stop the world and step off, but before you do, you want to sell out. Let's take a little inventory of you.

I once read a newspaper article about a lady who had a rash on her face. She went to the doctor, who prescribed some drugs that made her lose her sight. She was awarded a million dollars. Would you exchange places with this lady? You say you want to have more money, but here's a million dollars, and you're saying, "Not me."

I also read about a lady who was injured in an airplane accident, which broke her back. She was going to be flat on her back for the rest of her life. The insurance company gave her a million dollars. Would you exchange places with her? You say money is important, but you would not swap your health for that million dollars.

Betty Grable was a film star of the 1940s who was famed for her legs. They were insured for a million dollars. Would you like to see a million-dollar pair of legs right now? Look right down at your very own: there's a pair of million-dollar legs. Or is it $10 million or $110 million? How many of you would take a million dollars for your legs? If they'll even move you around at all, you know perfectly well the answer is an emphatic no.

Now we've got a million dollars for your eyes, a million for your back, and a million for your legs. That's $3 million already.

Do you already like yourself a little bit better than you did a few minutes ago? Your self-image is already growing, and that is as it should be.

Let's get practical as we take this inventory. I saw where a Rembrandt painting sold for in excess of $1 million. I thought to myself, "Boy, oh boy, that must be some kind of paint they put on that canvas," because I didn't realize it was that expensive. Then I got to thinking, "Maybe it's not just the paint or the canvas that is worth a million dollars. Maybe it's the arrangement that's on the canvas." I started thinking this thing through. Why would this painting be worth a million dollars? Because Rembrandt was a genius—a talent that comes along only once every 100 or 200 years. It was his genius that was being recognized and rewarded.

Then I thought about something else. There have been millions of paintings since the beginning of time, but this is the only painting in existence exactly like that one. It is an original. No other painting in existence is like it, and its very rarity gives it value.

Then I got to thinking about you. Since the beginning of time, billions of people have occupied the face of this earth. There is not now, there never has been, and there never will be another you. You're the rarest thing in existence. Because of your rarity, you surely have an enormous value. We know there never has been or will be another you, because if there had been, it would be an admission by God that he had made a mistake, and God can make no mistakes. It's your rarity that gives you this value.

Today computers are magnificent: it's incredible what some of them can do. They've got talking computers. Recently a wealthy West Texas oilman was talking to a computer in Houston. He stood in front of it and said, "I have in excess of 100,000 acres of land."

The computer said, "Man, that is a lot of dirt."

The fella said, "Not only that, but I've got 28,000 head of cattle."

The computer said, "Boy, that is a lot of bull."

The fella said, "Not only that, but I have and always keep in my possession in excess of $100,000 cash."

The computer mugged him.

Computers can do remarkable things, but even the most sophisticated computer can only store about 1/10,000 as much information as your brain. If scientists were to even attempt to create a computer that could compete with the human brain, it would require billions of dollars and a structure larger than the Empire State Building, cost astronomical sums of money, and require more electricity to run than a city of many thousands of people. Yet this manmade computer could not even originate a thought, which you can do instantly.

Some say, "If I'm so smart, how come I'm broke?" Well, my friend, it's not that you don't have it, it's that you don't use it. If there was an oil well on your property, but you did not know it, you would draw no financial benefit from it. If you had an enormous amount of ability but were unaware of it, you would never mine the gold mine or the oil well that's between your ears, which is infinitely more valuable than any gold mine.

The problem is that you came equipped with your mind at birth, and it was free. If I owned your mind, we'd both be better off, because I would sell it to you, let's say, for $100,000. I'd be much wealthier, but you too would be better off, because you would have made the bargain purchase of all time. Never again would you look in a mirror and say, "You stupid so-and-so." You would look in that mirror and say, "Man alive, you are really something. You are super. You're fantastic. You can do it. I know you can do it. You'd better: I've got 100,000 bucks tied up in you."

You spend thousands of dollars for an automobile, and if somebody says something ugly about it, you get powerful unhappy. If you buy a suit of clothes for hundreds of dollars, and somebody makes a catty remark about it, you don't like that either. Yet when people say derogatory things about us billion-dollar individuals, on many occasions we're inclined to agree with them. This does not make any sense.

The mind is a remarkable thing. When you utter a word, this computer of yours has to coordinate seventy-two muscles in exactly the right manner, or the word does not come out so that someone can understand you. Seventy-two muscles to utter one word!

Now that you've read this, do you like yourself better than you did five minutes ago?

The third reason you should like yourself better is very simply this: I saw a bumper sticker the other day that explains it completely. It said, "God loves you whether you like it or not." That's right.

Maybe you have small children, five or six years old. They come to you and say, "Mom, nobody likes me. I can't get along with anybody. I can't do anything. I'm a nothing, a nobody." Does that excite you? Do you say, "That's right, sweetheart. You're absolutely nothing, and I'm so glad you finally admit it"? Or does it tear your heart out when they say that?

How do you think Almighty God feels when we look up at him and say, "Lord, I'm a nothing. I'm a nobody." I think you're treading on dangerous territory. I've got a lot of courage, but I don't have enough courage to say to Almighty God, "You made a mistake when you put me on planet earth." The Bible says that we are created in God's own image: only "a little lower than the angels" (Psalm 8:5). The apostle Paul says someday we're going to judge those angels (1 Corinthians 6:3). When Paul wrote, "I can do all things through Christ which strengtheneth me" (Philemon 4:13), I don't think this is ego.

John 15:5 says, "I am the vine, and ye are the branches." When a man confidently expresses his capability, understanding that that capability is a God-given right and privilege of his, he is not bragging. He is expressing confidence in the source of his power. If we understand that, it makes all the difference in the world.

Singer Ethel Waters was at a Billy Graham revival in London, where there were thousands and thousands of people. Somebody came up to her and said, "How do you explain the fact that this man, Billy Graham, attracts so many people?"

Ethel, with that big beautiful smile and voice of hers, looked at him, grinned, and said, "Honey, God don't sponsor no flops."

If you're not as successful, if you're not as happy, if you're not accomplishing as much as you might like, maybe you have the wrong sponsor. Think about it for a moment. God designed us and put us here for a purpose. I cannot believe that he wants you or me to be broke or miserable any more than you want that little boy or little girl of yours to be miserable. God wants us to enjoy the good things. I believe I can show you scripture all day long to verify what I am saying.

Mary Crowley, a beautiful, enormously successful Christian businesswoman in Dallas, says, "You are somebody because God doesn't take time to make a nobody." Then she grins and says, "God made man, took one look, said, 'I can do better than that,' and made woman." So when you take inventory, you've got to like yourself better.

How do you build your self-image? Dress up. I've noticed that that red-headed sugar baby of mine goes to the beauty parlor every Wednesday. Now I don't know exactly everything that takes place down there: all they do is rearrange some hair on her head. But when she comes home, she's excited, she's enthused, she's motivated. If you're a woman, how do you feel when you come back from the beauty parlor? All they do is rearrange the hair on your head, but don't you feel more excited? Aren't you prettier? Don't you like yourself more? Aren't you more confident?

Make up and dress up if you want to go up. Girls, when you go to a party and everybody else is dressed formally but you're wearing a pair of slacks, how do you feel? Don't you stand smaller? You stay in the corners, and you don't want anybody to see you. You're terribly insecure and uncomfortable because you know that your appearance is not quite in keeping with the occasion.

We can prove beyond any doubt that if little Johnny and Mary have on a new outfit that they're proud of when they go to school, they do better work and their conduct is better as a result. The same is true for the worker: when we dress up, our self-esteem is definitely increased. They did a series in Dallas at a home for the aged. The average age of the women was eighty-three. A company came in and gave them facials on a regular basis. When these women got their faces made up, the director of the institute said that their enthusiasm was much greater. They perked up, they acted younger, they felt better, and many of their physical ailments disappeared. If you want to improve your image, just dress up. That is one way you can do it.

Another way to build your image: read Horatio Alger stories. There's no way that you could read the stories of Walter Chrysler, Henry Ford, Abraham Lincoln, or Booker T. Washington without being tremendously motivated and inspired. It's the same old routine: "They did it, so I can too."

Read the story of Eartha White. The daughter of an ex-slave, she made millions of dollars in Jacksonville, Florida, and gave all the money to the development and furtherance of her people. You look at this and say, "If at that time of extreme racial prejudice, the daughter of an ex-slave could accomplish all of this, then I can too."

Read the stories in the Bible over and over, because this will build your self-image. Want to build your image? Listen to good, motivational talks and recordings. Listen to the W. A. Criswells, the Kenneth McFarlands, and the Robert Schullers. Listen to the Dexter Yagers. Dexter, in my judgment, has it put together more completely from a financial and spiritual point of view than any other speaker that I know personally.

Would you like to build your self-confidence? Build it the way they do in school. You take a child and you teach them that 2 times 2 is 4. As soon as they learn that, they learn that 3 times 3 is 9, and 4 times 4 is 16. As they gain confidence in the simple things, their confidence grows for more complex things.

A high jumper who wants to jump six feet starts out by setting the bar at considerably less than that. He jumps at a lower height, and that builds his confidence. Then he moves it up a little bit, and then a little more. In the game of life, it's exactly the same thing. The little girl who wants to learn how to cook starts out with a simple batch of oatmeal cookies. Then she gets a little fancier as she goes along and develops confidence.

I was in the sales training world for many years, in the cookware business. If a salesman ever got in a slump, in most cases it indicated a loss of confidence. He could not sell a big-ticket item, so we would give him a smaller, less expensive item to sell. He would sell a couple of those, and he'd say, "I've got my confidence back. I'm getting the momentum back." Then he would go back to selling more and more. Harvard psychologist David McClelland calls this process *accomplishment feedback*.

To build your self-image, join the smile and compliment club. It's impossible to smile at somebody and have them smile back without feeling better as a result. It's impossible to pay somebody a compliment without receiving a benefit as a direct result. Do you want to feel better? Make somebody else feel better. Again, you can get everything in life that you want if you will help enough other people get what they want.

Let me tell you about one of the great boosters that I continually use. If you ever call my house, I answer by saying, "Oh, good morning to you." Or I might say, "Hidy, hidy, hidy." Or "Hello, we're having a super day at the Ziglars' and hope you are too."

You might say, "Ziglar, why do you answer the telephone like that?" Very simple: that's the way I feel. And if I feel that way, why should I not express it on the telephone? Many times, people have said, "Boy, I'm glad I called you. I feel better already because you answered the telephone the way you did."

When I answer the telephone that way, two things happen: I immediately feel better, and the other person immediately feels better. In the business I'm in, if they've called to buy something, I don't believe that that's going to hurt my sales efforts. If they've called to sell me something, it gives me an excellent chance to get my commercial in first.

The Bible says, "This is the day which the Lord hath made; we will rejoice and be glad in it" (Psalm 118:24). So why shouldn't I feel that way? Make somebody feel better. It makes you feel better. This builds your self-image.

Let me give you a personal family experience. Some years ago, my youngest daughter wanted a job. She couldn't find one anywhere except in a cafeteria. I don't know if you've ever worked in a cafeteria line; I never gave it much thought until she got that job. But I'll tell you, that's the most difficult, most thankless job that I've ever witnessed. If she tried to rush the customers along, they got unhappy. If she didn't rush them along, management was unhappy. If she gave the customers as much as they wanted, management was unhappy. If she didn't give them as much as they wanted, they were unhappy. If she was friendly and talked to them, some of them figured she was being too assertive and got unhappy. Others wanted her to talk with them.

It's a difficult situation. Of the people who go down a cafeteria line, 99.99 percent treat the girls as machinery. I never gave this any thought until my own daughter was involved. Today I never go down a cafeteria line without speaking enthusiastically to every person there: "How are you doing? Isn't it a beautiful day? That's a great-looking salad. My, that's good-looking chicken; I believe I'll have some of that." Some of them look at me in absolute shock: they've never seen anything like that. But by the time I've been in a cafeteria about five or six times, it creates somewhat of a problem, because every last girl on the line starts piling the stuff on my plate.

Now that's not the reason I do it, but it does show that I feel better because the other person feels better. You can't build up another person without building yourself. It's absolutely impossible. Again, you can get everything in life you want if you will just help enough other people get what they want. This is the most practical psychology that has ever been taught. The Bible teaches it by saying, "Whatsoever a man soweth, that shall he also reap" (Galatians 6:7).

Do something for somebody who cannot do anything in return: this is an excellent way to build your self-image. My wife taught a functional illiterate how to read. He was due to graduate from high school, but when she started with him, he was reading at a second- or third-grade level. Why was he a functional illiterate? Very simple: they'd been passing him from one grade to the next. He would have graduated while still being unable to read. My wife brought this boy, whose name was Earl, up to a sixth- or seventh-grade level, which is not a tremendous thing for a high-school graduate, but it was infinitely better than it had been.

What could this boy do for my wife? Not a thing in the world. Or could he? When she came home, she was motivated and excited. She would say, "Honey, Earl has got a good mind; he's got an excellent memory; he has a good grasp of things. He simply did not know how to read." It made her feel much better, and her self-image improved as a result.

A long time ago, Charles Dickens said, "No one is useless in this world who lightens the burden of another." Build your self-image by doing exactly that. Want to build your self-image? Visit a shut-in. Go to see somebody in the hospital. Spend some time with an orphan. Take a homeless child out to the ball game. Do some things for somebody who cannot do anything in return. Become a volunteer for the Red Cross. Go out to the mental hospital and spend some time with the people there. The results will be tremendous.

There's something that is very important here: you must not do anything for a person that can do something back in return. This won't build your self-image. Furthermore, you've got to keep it a secret. If everybody knows what you're doing, its value is negated. Let it be your own individual accomplishment, your own secret.

Want to build your self-image? Get into the sales world. Now I'm going to be the first to admit I'm highly prejudiced on this one. I've been in the world of selling for decades. I have seen people get into this world who were so timid they could not lead a group in silent prayer. Six weeks later, I have seen the same people become astonishingly enthusiastic. They even get up in front of some groups and lead them in singing. They do an amazing number of things, because their image and confidence have been built up.

The sales world is a very positive world. In it, people are saying, "You can do it, you can do it," instead of "You can't."

I believe that America would be a stronger, richer, better, more prosperous and progressive nation if every public official—elected or appointed—had to come to an enthusiastic sales meeting every morning and let some of that enthusiasm and optimism rub off on them. They would become so excited that they would do an infinitely better job.

To build your self-image, be around enthusiastic, progressive people. As I said earlier, you become part of what you're around: you acquire the characteristics and habits of others. For example, I'm sure you've noticed that you can take a Southern boy or a Southern girl and send them up north, and in a matter of months they acquire an accent. Or you can take a Northern boy or girl and send them down south, and in a matter of months we have them talking normally.

To build your self-image, make a list of your positive qualities. Put down the things about you that you know are good and keep that list. Ask your friends to give you a list of the things they like about you. Tell them, "Don't you dare tell me anything you don't like. Just give me a list of the things that you do like about me."

You might even get to be like this old boy down home. He's walking down the street, talking to himself. One of his friends says, "John, how come you're talking to yourself?"

"For two reasons. First of all, I like to talk to intelligent people. Second, I like to listen to intelligent people talk." With that kind of self-image, I would say that he's in pretty good shape.

Another way to build your self-image: make a victory list. In your life, you've done a lot of things that you are proud of, but you've never made a list of them. If you made an A in a tough course, if you whipped the school bully, if you led the parade one week, if you did anything that you are proud of, make a list.

See, what you're deciding is very simple. You're deciding, "Hey, I'm for me, not against me." When things are not going well, you take your victory list out and you say, "Boy, oh boy, this is really something. Look at all the things I've done in the past. Any woman or any man who's done all of these things can't be all bad." As you look at a list of these accomplishments, your self-image continues to build.

In order to build your self-image, there are some things you must avoid. You must avoid pornography. Psychologically, it is impossible to watch mankind at its very worst without having it affect you in the process. I have been told that psychologically, when you view a *Deep Throat* or a *Last Tango in Paris* three times, it has the equivalent effect of having the physical experience one time. You cannot see humanity at its worst without having it affect you.

Avoid the daily soap operas. I have not seen more than two minutes of a soap opera in twenty-five years. We've never permitted them in our house. To begin with, I have it on good authority they are getting more risqué. In addition, they're terribly negative. I challenge you: spend three minutes watching one. Without exception, in every single case, the hero either is in trouble, is headed for trouble, or has just gotten out of trouble. Now life just isn't that tough. Furthermore, we relate to what we see. Did you know that two-thirds of medical students acquire the symptoms of the disease they study? We see a situation on that screen day after day, pick out the one that most closely parallels ours, and say, "Yeah, I know exactly how she feels. That's the way my John done me, the dirty dog."

Every destructive habit starts slowly and gradually, and before you're aware that you've got the habit, the habit has got you. I've never talked to an alcoholic who started out to be one. I've never talked to a drug addict who started out to be one. They end up that way because they started somewhere.

Educators will tell you to get an education. They will say, "You should get a high school diploma. Get a college degree, because you'll earn more money if you do." They stress the value of an education. They say, "What you get out of books is tremendously important." Then they turn around and say, "Don't worry about censorship, because what could you possibly get out of a book that would hurt you?"

Think it through. A cup can contain either cool water to quench my thirst or poison that would kill me. What's in a book can build humankind or destroy humankind. To deliberately feed your mind with the wrong things is destructive to your self-image.

If you want to build your image, I think you need to go to school about failures. I think failures can teach us a great deal. For example, baseball great Hank Aaron has struck out more times than over 90 percent of the ballplayers who ever entered the major leagues. Most of us don't think of Hank as being a failure, though, do we? Babe Ruth struck out more times than any man in the history of the game; we don't think of him as a failure. Ty Cobb was thrown out trying to steal base more than any runner in the history of the game, but most of us don't think of Ty Cobb as a failure. Thomas Edison failed 14,000 times at one experiment. Bob Devaney was a high-school football coach at the age of forty-five but retired as the winningest college coach in football history. When Vince Lombardi was forty-four years old, he was still a line coach at Fordham University. I don't think you'd consider Albert Einstein a failure, but he did fail in math; so did Wernher von Braun. I don't think you'd think of singer Enrico Caruso as a failure, but for months his teacher tried to get him to quit singing, because every time he hit a high note his voice would break.

Every one of these people—including Walt Disney, who went broke seven times and had one nervous breakdown before he made it—failed and failed, but they learned something tremendously important. They learned that the only difference between a big shot and a little shot is that a big shot is just a little shot that kept shooting.

Another suggestion for building your self-image: take a public speaking course, or get up in front of a group and express yourself. The ability to get up in front of a group and express yourself does more to build your confidence than virtually anything I have ever encountered. I cannot overstress the importance of putting yourself into a position where you can talk to others in a group situation.

All of these steps in building a healthy self-image are designed to help you accept yourself. Once you do, it's no longer a matter of life and death to have others accept you. Once *you* like you, it doesn't matter as much whether others do or not. At that point, you will be not only accepted but welcomed by others. The reason is very simple: they will be accepting the real you, and the real you is so much nicer than the phony conformist who tries to please others and go along with the crowd.

When the real you is accepted, a lot of things happen. Your conduct changes for the better. Your morals pole-vault upward. Many of your little tensions disappear because you are secure within yourself, where security really lies. The little things that formerly bothered you no longer bother you at all. You don't sweat the small stuff. Your account in the bank of self-confidence will grow. Communication barriers will be removed, and your family relationships will improve, not only between husband and wife, but between parents and children.

Once you've accepted yourself, it's much easier to accept other people. Now I said *accept*. I didn't say that you are necessarily going to agree with other people. It does mean that you can accept and maybe even understand why they feel the way they do. When that happens, you will find it easier to get along with other people almost regardless of who they are.

In many cases, a person who fails to gain sufficient acceptance and recognition will start making adjustments and compromises. In fact, they may begin to act like somebody else. But if you can't make it as yourself, do you really think you can make it by being somebody else? You make a lousy anybody else, but you're the best *you* on the face of this earth.

If you don't accept yourself, you're inclined to want everybody else to accept you. But when you accept yourself, you're not destroyed if somebody else doesn't. Shakespeare said it extremely well: "This above all, to thine own self be true, / And it must follow, as the night the day, / Thou canst not then be false to any man."

Once you accept yourself for your true worth, symptoms such as vulgarity, profanity, obesity, sloppiness, promiscuity, and so forth will invariably disappear.

Look at the drug problem. Almost without exception, I've noticed that the boys and girls who get involved with drugs do not like themselves as they are. They're seeking a change, so they try to make it chemically, confusing and in many cases destroying themselves in the process.

I'm going to close this chapter with a challenge. It's in the form of an analogy.

The Japanese raise a beautiful tree called the bonsai, which grows to a height of something like eighteen inches. The bonsai tree is perfectly formed in every way, but it is a miniature. Go with me out to the soil of California, and you will see a giant sequoia or a giant redwood reaching hundreds of feet into the air. One of them is the General Sherman. The General Sherman reaches 271 feet high. It is so big in circumference that they could drive automobiles through it. If they were to cut it down and saw it into lumber, it would be enough to build thirty-five five-room houses.

The bonsai and the General Sherman at one time were exactly the same size. Each weighed less than 1/10,000 of an ounce, but the bonsai was planted in a little secluded spot. When it first made its appearance, the Japanese removed the tree by the roots. They tied off the feeder roots and the taproots. They deliberately stunted its growth.

The General Sherman, on the other hand, grew up in the rich soil of California. Nourished by the chemicals in the soil, the rain, and the sunshine, it grew into the magnificent forest giant that it is today. One tree had its growth goal stymied; the other had its growth encouraged.

You as an individual can make a choice: you can either become a bonsai tree or a General Sherman. The choice is yours.

As explained earlier, I have five major objectives here:

1. To demonstrate the importance of a healthy self-image.
2. To identify the causes of a poor self-image.

3. To reveal the manifestations of a poor self-image.

4. To give you some methods for improving your self-image.

5. To encourage you to choose and remain on the road to a healthy self-image.

Remember that nobody can make you feel inferior without your permission. I'm convinced now that you're in a position to refuse that permission to anyone. As you imagine the stairway to the top, there you are, on that self-image step. You're moving out of the crowd at the bottom. As time goes by, let me urge you, if any doubts enter your mind, if you encounter any difficulties in any area of your life, to return to this material, because this is the key to what's going to happen in your future, and you do have a beautiful one.

The Chinese have a saying: "A journey of a thousand leagues begins with a single step." Most people never get anywhere in life because they never start anywhere. You have started. You've taken the first giant step towards going all the way to the top. Keep on doing exactly what you are now doing, and I will see you at the top.

4

My Story

At this point, I'm going to tell you my story. I'm going to do this because I believe that my story is in fact your story. I don't believe that anyone will ever encounter this material who has been as despondent, as discouraged and down in the dumps, or who has threatened to quit as many times as I have.

I don't care who you are. I don't care where you live. I don't care what you've done or what you're doing. I honestly believe that I have already walked in your shoes. I believe I know your feelings. I believe I've already felt them. I believe I've already lived them. As I tell this story, I am not going to embellish it in any way. To the best of my ability, I'm going to communicate it to you exactly as it happened to me.

I was raised in a Mississippi town named Yazoo City. It's an incredible place. Even though it's small, it has produced the former president of the American Medical Association, the former president of the American Bar Association, the former president of the Southern Baptist Convention, the former chancellor of the University of North Carolina, the former editor of *Harper's* magazine, and the beloved country comedian Jerry Clower.

I've paid for every stitch of clothing I've ever owned or worn since before I was ten years old. I started working in a grocery store on the Saturday before I entered the fifth grade. I worked. I worked after school and on Saturdays all the way through high school. I used to be a teller. Now don't get hung up on that particular title. That just meant that I told people to move while I swept.

When I was a boy, my mother used to bake biscuits that were about three times as large as the ones you see today.

When I came home from school, I would take one of those biscuits, poke my finger into the center, pour molasses in it, and eat it. Those were our sweets in those days.

The store where I worked had a mammoth barrel of molasses. One day a little fellow came in, looked around, and didn't see the boss. He took the top off that barrel of molasses, ran his finger through the molasses, and popped it in his mouth. The boss made his appearance suddenly, grabbed the little fellow, swatted him across the bottom and said, "Boy, don't you ever let me see you do that again. Now you get out of here."

About a month later, the little fellow had apparently forgotten about the swat across the bottom and remembered how good the molasses was. He went back in the store, looked around, didn't see the boss, and went to that barrel of molasses. He ran his fingers through it again. Up popped the boss, and this time he really dusted him a couple of times and said, "Boy, don't you ever let me see you do that again!" The boy made his disappearance.

A sweet tooth is a terrible thing. A month later, the boy was there again and didn't see the boss anywhere. Again, he took that top off and, just as he ran his finger through the molasses, up popped the boss. This time, the boss didn't say a single word. He raced down, grabbed the little boy by the seat of his britches, lifted him up, and dropped him right in that barrel of molasses. As he was sinking out of sight, you could hear him praying, "Oh, Lord, give me the tongue to equal this opportunity."

On the serious side, it's been my prayer that I'll be given the tongue to deliver a psychology, a philosophy, a way of life that will have a bearing on your life.

I was working in that grocery store when I left Yazoo City in 1944. The war was on. The night before I left, the boss said, "Zig, I want to have a Dutch uncle talk with you, heart to heart. When the war is over"—and it was about over then—"I want you to come back and work for me in the market here."

I couldn't get excited about that, because at that time I was working over seventy hours a week and earning about $30. In 1944, things were different than they are today, but still, this just wasn't that much money.

The boss said, "Zig, I'll tell you what I'll do. If you'll come back and work for me two years, I'll teach you everything I know about running a market. I will then help you get set up with your own market."

He showed me that the year before, after taxes and expenses, he had netted $5,117. I could not believe that anybody in Yazoo City in 1943 could earn $5,117, so I was motivated. I was going to come back to Yazoo City when it was over, get a market, and earn $5,117 in a single year.

But during the war, I met that redhead and fell in love with her. We got married. When I was discharged, we went to the University of South Carolina. I worked my way through school and supported my wife by selling sandwiches, coffee cakes, milk, and coffee around the dormitories at night. During the winter months, business was excellent, but during the summer months, it was lousy.

First of all, there was only a four-day school week. Second, dormitories were not air-conditioned, and in that hot weather, most of the students wanted to go out at night to relax and get a little better refreshment. Business dropped to almost zero.

My wife was reading the paper one day, and she saw an ad for a salesman for $10,000, which we felt was more than just a coincidence. I say it was more than a coincidence because they wanted a $10,000 salesman, and we wanted the $10,000.

I called them and went down for an interview. When the interview was over, I was really motivated. I got back home and said, "Sweetheart, we're going to be earning $10,000 a year."

"Good. When do we start?"

"The man said he'd call me." I was so naive that I believed that when somebody said they were going to do something, they would do it. I believed then, as I believe now, that a man's word is an unbreakable contract: when you say something, that is the way it is.

I waited expectantly for the phone call for over a month. It did not come, so I wrote the man a letter saying, "I want the job. I need the job. I'm willing to work."

The man wrote me back and he said, "I'm sorry. We don't think you can sell."

I called him and said, "Why don't you just give me a chance? At least talk with me again." It took me one more month to persuade him that he should at least put me through a training school and see how I did.

This was a commission job, selling cookware on a person-to-person basis. It was on a commission, and I had to buy my own samples. There was no way this man had anything to lose, but he did not believe that I could sell. For the next two and a half years, all I did was prove that he had been right to start with.

Don't misunderstand. That does not mean that I didn't sell a lot, because I did. I sold my furniture. I sold my car. That's so close to the truth that it is not as funny as it might be.

Let me tell you what I've done a thousand times. I've done exactly the same thing that you may have done in your business or career. I've knocked on a lot of doors, praying that nobody was going to answer. I've dialed a telephone many times, and the most exciting sound I could get was a busy signal.

I have actually done this: I have had a prospect right in front of me, a prospect a block away, and a prospect five miles away. What would I do? Obviously, I'd drive over to the prospect five miles away. I justified it by saying, "I'm planning what I'm going to say." Or by saying, "They're probably having lunch or dinner, or the baby's asleep, or the husband's asleep, or this is not the right time." A thousand things went through my mind, but the truth is, I did not want to talk to anybody for fear of rejection.

As a young salesman, I did some things that almost defy belief. Many times, I've had to leave a grocery line because I'd miscalculated, and I had to put back a can of beans. When my first daughter was born, the hospital bill was $64. I did not have the $64. I had to get out and sell two sets of cookware to get my own daughter out of the hospital. I know what it is to be broke. I have often bought 50 cents' worth of gasoline at a time.

Eventually I got a trainer to go out with me on a sales call and see what my problem was. After it was over, I asked, "Bill, what do you think?"

"Zig, let me ask you a question."

"OK."

"What are you selling?"

"Now, Bill, you know perfectly well what I'm selling."

"Sure. I know what you're selling, but don't you think you should have told that lady?"

"Bill, it wasn't that bad."

"Zig, I'll guarantee she had no earthly idea of what you were selling. Let's go to the training room."

We went to the training room, which had a recording machine, and recorded a twenty-one-minute sales presentation. By actual count, I had 187 "ahhs" in the talk. If you put your pencil to it, that figures out to nine "ahhs" per minute. Today I'm known as the fastest drawl in the West, yet there I was, with 187 "ahhs" in a twenty-one-minute sales presentation.

I stuck along with it to survive. If I had sense, I would have quit. If in the early years my mother had not taught me the merits of perseverance, giving something your very best and not letting every breeze that comes along blow you aside, I undoubtedly would have quit right then and there.

At that time, my company started putting on cooking demonstrations. A lot of people would come in, you would cook up a meal, and serve them the food. I wanted to do that, but I had two problems. The first problem was, I'd never seen a demonstration and had no earthly idea how to cook. The second problem was, I didn't have any money to buy the groceries.

With the confidence that generally goes with ignorance, I figured I could overcome the first one: I could learn how to cook a meal by reading a book, but what about the groceries?

I had heard of a Mrs. B. C. Moore, who lived at 2210 High Street in Columbia, South Carolina. She had bought the cookware but did not like it because she did not know how to use it. I went over to Mrs. Moore and I did a sales job. I said, "Mrs. Moore, I'll make a deal with you. I'll teach you how to use that set of cookware if you will invite some prospects in to see the demonstration and if you will buy the food."

"OK, I'll do it."

I will never forget it. On the night of the demonstration, we had a Mr. and Mrs. B. C. Moore, a Mr. and Mrs. Clarence Spence, and a Dr. and Mrs. Gay. I guess the demonstration was all right; at least I didn't burn anything. When I finished demonstrating, Mrs. Spence said, "You know, that is really nice, and we sure do need something to cook in. But now is the wrong time. We've just had this bill and that problem." Then she went on, "But I've always got bills, I've always got expenses, and I promised myself the next time I had a chance to buy a good set of cookware, I was going to buy it. I'll take a set."

Mrs. Gay went through exactly the same song and dance, giving every reason why she shouldn't buy it, but she said the same thing: "I think I'll take it."

Think about this: You are the salesman. You're dead broke, you are working on a commission, and you've got two ladies who are saying, "I'll take it." What would you have done at that moment?

Guess what Old Zig did, and I give you my word: this is exactly what happened. I looked at my watch and said, "Ladies, I'd like the best in the world to sell you the set of cookware, but I can't, because I've got another appointment in five minutes, and I'm running late right now." With two ladies with the money in their hot little hands saying, "I'll take it," I said, "Oh, no. You won't either, because I've got something important to do."

I walked out on them wanting to buy it, and the people I was going to see were not home.

Of course, the next day I did come back, and they did buy. But would you in your dumbest, greenest day ever have done such an idiotic thing as that? I think anybody with sense enough to get out of a telephone booth without written directions would never have done that.

All I'm trying to say to you, my friend, is, whoever you are, wherever you are, and whatever you're doing, there is hope for you.

Then one day, in one twenty-four-hour period, the entire ball game turned completely around. I went to a meeting in Charlotte, North Carolina, on Monday and all day long learned absolutely nothing that I remember. That night I had a demonstration. I got home at 11:30 that night, very tired, but the baby kept me up most of the rest of the night.

At 5:30 the next morning, the alarm clock sounded, and by force of habit, I rolled out of bed. We were living in a small three-room apartment above a grocery store. I cracked the venetian blinds and looked at a street light fifteen feet away. You could see the snow filtering down, and there were twelve inches of snow on the ground. I was driving a Crosley automobile without a heater, so I did what any intelligent human being would do: I got back in bed.

But as I lay down, two thoughts occurred to me: I never missed a meeting; I'd never even been late for one. And my mother had raised me on one basic philosophy: "Son, if you're in something, get in it. If you're not in it, get out of it." The Bible says, "I would thou wert cold or hot. So then because thou art lukewarm, and neither cold nor hot, I will spue thee out of my mouth" (Revelation 3:15–16).

As I lay there in that bed, I realized that I had to get up and go to that meeting. I went, and my entire world turned around that day. I still didn't learn a lot. But when it was done, Mr. Merrell, the man conducting the meeting, took me aside. He said, "Zig, I've been watching you for two and a half years since you've been in this company, and I have never seen such a waste."

Now that'll get your attention, and it sure got mine. I said, "Mr. Merrell, what do you mean?"

"You've got an enormous amount of ability. You can go all the way to the top. You could be a national champion. You could be a great one if you just believed in yourself and went to work."

I never heard words like that before in my life. I was a little guy in school. When I was a senior in high school, I weighed less than 120 pounds fully dressed. I never dated a girl until after I was seventeen years old, and that was a blind date somebody else had gotten for me. I'd always seen myself as the little guy from the little town who someday was going to go back to that little town, open his own meat market, and earn $5,117 in a single year. Now here was a man saying, "You could be a great one if you would just believe in yourself and go to work."

I had a demonstration that night, for which I'll always be grateful. I believe God arranged it purposefully, because we had three couples there, and they did not have a chance. If they had been even half smart, they would have walked in and said, "Look, Ziglar, forget the sales talk. We'll take it right now, because we know that we're going to buy."

I still hadn't learned anything else about selling, but I was convinced that they were going to buy. My whole attitude changed, because my image had changed. I'd never heard anybody say I could be a great one. I believed Mr. Merrell. I don't know if he was really sincere or not (he later became a close friend of mine and assured me that he was), but the important thing is that I believed what he said. Before the year was over, I was the number two salesman in America out of over 7,000.

I swapped the Crosley for a luxury car. I had the finest promotion the company had. The next year, I was the highest paid manager in the United States. Three years later, I became the youngest divisional supervisor in the company's sixty-six-year history.

I'm convinced beyond any reasonable doubt that the only thing that actually happened was the fact that I had taken a different look at myself. When your self-image changes and you begin to see yourself in the proper light, you are going to perform exactly the same way.

You cannot perform beyond what you think you are capable of doing. Positive thinking does not work for many people because they don't believe they deserve success. They don't believe they're entitled to it. They don't have the proper image of themselves. If you don't think you deserve it, you're simply not going to get it.

I tell this story in such detail because, as I said earlier, I believe the story is your story. I believe that the greatest thing that you can ever do for anybody is not to give them part of what you've got, but to reveal to them what they've got. According to Harvey Firestone, founder of the tire company, you get the best out of others when you give the best of yourself. Many people have gone a lot further than they thought they could because somebody else thought they could.

I tell the story of my own life and personal experiences because they exemplify the importance of self-image. Growth came about because somebody else looked down and said, "You are a great one."

Yet again, I believe deeply and completely that you can get everything in life that you want if you'll just help enough other people get what they want. I never talk to any group anywhere until I have first asked God to make me a P. C. Merrell. I once heard a man who hires speakers say that many speakers say or think they're going to change the world. He said, "Those guys are crazy. You're not going to change the world when you get up and make a speech."

If, deep down in my heart, I did not believe that I was going to change the world for somebody, I would never get up to make a talk. I believe the spoken word is one of the most potent weapons ever designed by man, for good or, improperly used, for evil. Words that paint a picture of success and gratification, of accomplishment, that persuade you that you can go more places, do more things, be better and have more, are words that will be tremendously beneficial to you. As we make this transition from building a healthy self-image into your relationship with others, let me again say that if you buy these ideas and do these things, then you're moving up the stairway to the top.

5

Your Relations with Others

The following two chapters have four purposes:

1. To clarify the way you should see other people.
2. To sell the concept that you treat other people as you see them.
3. To establish that you can get everything in life you want if you will just help enough other people get what they want.
4. To identify genuine love and give specific suggestions on how to court after you're married.

The last purpose might seem a little odd. But if you are not married, the chances are good that someday you will be. Whether or not you ever will be, it's important to know how to deal with members of the other sex.

I was doing some recording once, and a little lady came up to me. I smiled, and she said, "You're Zig, aren't you?"

"Yeah."

"You're going to do some recording tonight, aren't you?"

"Yeah."

"You're scared, aren't you?"

"No. I'm excited about it. I'm enthused. I'm turned on. I'm motivated."

"You're scared."

"No, I'm not scared. I'm enthusiastic. I'm motivated."

"You're scared."

"I am not scared, and I can't understand why you're trying to get me to say I'm scared when obviously I'm not."

"If you're not scared, what are you doing here in the ladies' room?"

I always like to talk to ladies. Women are so much more practical than men—like this lady down home. A bum came up to her and said, "Ma'am, would you give me 50 cents for a sandwich?"

"Not until I've seen the sandwich."

You see, that's practical—like the two girls who were talking. One of them said, "I didn't want to marry a man for his money, but that was the only way I could get it." You see, that's practical.

A couple of old boys down home went out deer hunting, and they got lucky and killed an eighteen-point buck. Now that's a lot of deer. One of them had him by one hind leg, another one had him by the other hind leg, and they were dragging him through the woods.

Pretty soon they met another deer hunter. He was a veteran; he hadn't killed anything, but he was full of good advice. He said, "Congratulations on killing that big buck; that's some deer. But you're pulling him by his hind legs, so his horns are getting caught in the brush. If you reverse that and pull him by the horns, you'll pull him so much easier, and it won't be half as much trouble."

The men turned and started pulling the buck by the horns. They'd pulled him about a hundred yards when one of them said, "You know, that old boy was right. This deer is a lot easier to pull this way. That old boy is one smart cookie."

The other one said, "I don't think he's so smart. Look, we're getting further from the car all the time."

As we make the transition from you and your healthy self-image into relationships with others, let me emphasize that we do not go through life by ourselves.

Several years ago, there was a survey done of 100 self-made millionaires in New York City. The study disclosed some astonishing facts. These millionaires varied in age from twenty-one to seventy years of age. Their education levels varied all the way from grade school to one fellow who had two or three PhDs. Interestingly, nearly 70 percent of them came from cities of less than 15,000 people.

There were many differences among these self-made millionaires, but all of them had one common characteristic: they had the capacity to look at a person or situation and regardless of how bad or negative it might be, see something good in it. They emphasized the good and not the negative.

One day a little boy had a falling-out with his mother and said to her in anger, "I hate you. I hate you." Then, realizing what he had said, he made a mad dash for the front door, figuring that mama was going to get on him a little bit.

They lived over a little valley, and as he ran out, the little boy let that anger come out, screaming, "I hate you. I hate you."

The echo came back from the valley: "I hate you. I hate you."

Somewhat frightened, the little boy ran back to his mother and said, "Mother, there's a mean little boy out in the valley who says he hates me."

His mother said, "Well, son, why don't you go back out and see if you can find another little boy? Why don't you say out loud, 'I love you. I love you'?"

The little boy ran out, and this time he shouted, "I love you. I love you." The echo came back, "I love you. I love you."

Life is an echo. The Good Book says that as you sow, so also shall you reap. Whatever you plant—I don't care what it is or where it is—is going to come back to you.

I have a belief, and I hope to be able to substantiate it rather strongly: you treat people exactly as you see them. I'm also convinced beyond a reasonable doubt that if you want to find something good in a person or a situation, all you've got to do is look for that good.

Once in Dallas, I was introduced to a fantastic man named Walter Hailey. He was at one of the mammoth affiliated warehouse stores, and he had conceived of a new idea for selling insurance through grocery stores. They were doing extraordinarily well.

When I met Walter, we related to each other. I guess he was trying to sell me something and I was trying to sell him something, yet we really had nothing to sell each other. But he said, "Zig, I got an idea I'd like to share with you, and I want you to see it." So we went over to the warehouse.

When he walked in past the switchboard operator, Walter said, "Zig, excuse me, just a moment." He went over to the operator and said, "You know, I've been meaning to tell you that I think you're one of the greatest guys on the telephone I have ever seen. You really make people feel that you are delighted that they have seen fit to dial this number."

The little guy was grinning from ear to ear and said, "Thank you, Mr. Hailey. I try to be pleasant."

We walked on in. As we walked through an open door, Walter said to me, "Excuse me, Ziglar; step in here just for a second."

He walked into that department to a man there, stuck his hand out, introduced himself, and said, "I have not had the privilege of meeting you personally, but I'm very familiar with your department. Since you've taken over this department, we have not had a single complaint."

The man smiled and said, "Mr. Hailey, I really appreciate your saying that. I enjoy this work, and I do the very best I can."

We walked on upstairs into the insurance office, and as we did, he said, "Zig, I want to introduce you to the greatest secretary that ever sat behind a typewriter." And he said to her, "Little lady, you know, my wife thinks you hung the moon and you can take it down at your pleasure." He added, "I'm asking you right now as a personal favor: don't take it down."

The secretary smiled and said, "Well, you sure do have a sweet wife, Mr. Hailey, and I really appreciate your making that comment."

We walked in to the office where the insurance man was, and Mr. Hailey said to me, "Zig, shake hands with the greatest insurance man to ever put on a pair of shoes."

The man stood up and said, "Man, that is some kind of compliment, and I accept it at face value," and we laughed.

The entire trip took less than two minutes, but there were four people. I ask you, what was the net result for those four people that day? Do you think they were more productive or less productive? Do you think they worked with more excitement, more enthusiasm, more zest? If they were on your payroll and you said something like that, do you think you would get better results that day? You'd better believe that you'd get much better results.

You might say, "Well, Ziglar, were those compliments sincere?" I believe that they were: as I watched Walter Hailey pass them out, I became completely convinced that they were very sincere compliments. Some people say that compliments are just so much air, but for that matter, the tires on our automobiles are just filled with so much air. But there is no doubt that they ease us along life's highway much more comfortably.

A number of years ago at Harvard University, Dr. Robert Rosenthal conducted a series of intriguing experiments with three groups of students and three groups of rats. He called the first group of students together and said, "You're in luck. You've got the genius rats. These rats are the smartest rats you've ever seen. They've been bred for intelligence. They're going to go down to the end of the maze in nothing flat. They're going to eat cheese like you've never seen rats eat cheese before. You'd better buy an extra supply, because these rats are smart. As a matter of fact, they're probably going to gain weight eating cheese."

Dr. Rosenthal went to the second group of students and said, "You got the average rats. They're not too bright, not too dumb, just average rats. Now you'd better buy some cheese, but don't expect too much from them, because they're average rats."

He went to the third group of students and said, "You've got a problem. These rats are idiots. They've been inbred for a number of generations, and it'll be amazing if any one of them ever gets down to the end of the maze."

For the next six weeks, under the most carefully controlled scientific conditions, the students ran a series of experiments with the rats. The genius rats performed like genius rats. They went down into the maze in nothing flat and ate lots of cheese.

The average rats—well, what do you expect from a bunch of average rats? It was an average performance. On occasions, they would get to the end of the maze, but it was no big deal; no records were broken.

And those idiot rats? Was that ever sad! Occasionally, one did get down to the end of the maze, but you knew it was an accident: they'd just stumbled into it; you had a distinct feeling that they would never do it again.

Here's the intriguing thing: There were no genius rats. There were no idiot rats. They were all average rats. As a matter of fact, they were all out of the same litter. Their difference in performance came about because of the difference in treatment, and the difference in treatment came about because of the difference in the way the students saw the rats.

Even though rats can't understand human talk and humans can't understand rat talk, there's apparently a communication of attitude and intent.

Let me ask you some questions: What kind of kids have you got? What kind of customers have you been calling on? What kind of neighbors do you have? What kind of husband do you have? What kind of wife do you have?

You might say, "Ziglar, wait just one minute. You're talking about rats one minute, the next minute my kids or my husband. You've got to be clearer than that."

Let's take a step further, because researchers did. They went to a school and said to one teacher, "You're in luck. You got the genius kids. All these kids are bright. Some of them are so bright, it's frightening. Why, they're going to be answering questions before you even ask them."

They told another teacher that the kids were lazy: "They're going to say, 'Oh, teacher. That's too hard. We could never learn that. We can't get it all done.'"

The researchers went to a third teacher and said, "You've got a bunch of average kids. Not too bright, not too dumb, just average kids. Don't expect too much, but do expect average results, because these are average kids."

At the end of one year, the genius students were one full year ahead of the average students, and I suspect that you're exactly five minutes ahead of me, aren't you? You're absolutely right: there were no genius students. They were all average students. The only difference was brought about by the difference in treatment, and the difference in treatment was brought about by the way the teachers saw them. You treat people the way you see them.

The researchers took the process one step further. They went to another school and said to the teacher, "There are five geniuses in your class," and they identified the five. "They're going to do tremendous work for you," they said. The class was in lecture format. All the students were in a large class. But would you believe that at the end of the year, those five stuck out like a sore thumb over the rest?

Why and how could this be? Very simple. Every time one of the "genius" students asked a question, the teacher would tell them, "There's no problem. You won't have any difficulty with that. You can do fantastic work. You are great." Because the teacher was always communicating this message, the students did a much better job.

John Wooden was the coach of the UCLA Bruins, who won ten of twelve national championships, including seven in a row. He had an intriguing philosophy. Yes, he was looking for a good athlete, but he was not just looking for a good athlete. He looked for a complete human being, and he was just as concerned with their morals and integrity as he was with their athletic ability.

He was a super nice guy, and he refutes Leo Durocher's old adage that nice guys always finish last. I might point out that Leo Durocher, in over twenty-five years of managing a major league team, had lots of experience in finishing last and never finishing first but once.

In short, when you look at people and you can see the good there, then you treat them accordingly. Now please don't misunderstand this: I'm not saying that regardless of how miserably a person performs, you are supposed to say that the performance is super. In fact, a study in San Francisco reveals one of the most horrendous problems in our country: when educators say to a student, "That's fantastic. That's super," when in reality it is a miserable performance, now we've got a student going all the way through school and the teacher is saying, "It's super," when in fact it was not. They are doing that because they don't want to take a little extra time and trouble to start teaching.

In short, you look at the performance. You can criticize the performance and say, "You can do better," but don't criticize the performer. Look at the performer and say, "You can do better than that." Look at the performance and say, "This is not up to your standards." That is the important distinction.

Once I was speaking in Lansing, Michigan. I was recuperating from surgery. My gallbladder had ruptured, which caused some problems. The doctor sewed me up. When he got through, he said, "Now, Zig, there's nothing wrong with your mouth, so you can go back to talking. But you can't pick anything up."

I got to Lansing after midnight, when the bellboys had all gone home. The night clerk was by himself. I had a big bag and a big box, and I said to the night clerk, "Man, I've got a problem. The doctor says I must not pick anything up. I'm recuperating from surgery. Can you help me?"

"The bellboy is gone, but yes, I can close the desk and take it up myself."

As we got on the elevator, I realized that I had a problem: I know how to treat bellboys. You go to the room, the bellboy flicks on the switch, and says, "Yep, it works." He sticks his hand out, you grease it, and everybody's happy. But how do you treat night clerks? I'd never dealt with a night clerk like that. If I tipped him, I ran the risk of having him get on his high horse and say, "I've got a big salary. I'm not the kind of employee you tip. You can thank me, but don't give me your tip. Keep your money." On the other hand, if I didn't tip him, he might say to himself, "What kind of guys do they have down in Dallas? Here I close my desk and lug the bag up to the room, and he didn't give me a buck. What a cheapskate."

As I say, you treat people exactly as you see them, but I didn't know how I saw him. Fortunately, as we were getting off the elevator, he clarified the situation. He casually mentioned to me that he was a student at the university. Now I had the strong suspicion that he wasn't desirous of informing me of his overwhelming ambition to acquire a higher education. I got the idea that he was really saying, "Look, friend, I'm working my way through school. If you want to put some money there, that's all right. You go ahead."

Now I saw him in a different light. I was relieved, because you treat people as you see them. I gave him the tip. He was happy; I was happy.

This happened many years ago at a mental institution outside of Boston. In those days, such institutions were not enlightened to any degree, although this particular one was rather special. They did treat their patients with care and concern and modern methods, as they were viewed in that day.

Nevertheless, this institution had a dungeon in which they put the hopelessly insane. In the dungeon there was a girl, and her name was Little Annie. There was nothing that could be done about Little Annie. She was an animal. Everybody agreed that she was hopeless.

At this time, there was an elderly nurse at this institution who was approaching her retirement years. Each day, she started going down into the dungeon and eating her lunch just outside of Little Annie's cage. Some days, Little Annie would ignore her. Some days, she wouldn't even speak to her. Some days, she would viciously try to get out of the cage, and on other days she would try to attack even the person who brought her food. Or she would be completely withdrawn.

One day, the elderly nurse baked some brownies and took them down to Little Annie. She said, "I'm outside the cage." When the nurse came back the next day, the brownies were gone. The next week, she did it again. The next week, she did it again. After just a few weeks, the doctors noticed a dramatic change in Little Annie. They moved her upstairs, and over a period of years, they were able to restore her to complete normalcy. One day, they said to her, "Little Annie, we've done everything that we can for you; you may go home now."

But Little Annie said, "I don't want to go. This institution has meant so much to me. I would like to learn everything that I can and be as much help as I can, out of gratitude to you and what you've done for me."

Many years later, Queen Victoria, while pinning England's highest award to a foreigner on Helen Keller, asked her, "To whom or to what do you owe your remarkable accomplishments in life?"

Helen Keller, without a moment's hesitation, said, "Had it not been for Little Annie Sullivan, you never would have heard of Helen Keller."

Actually, Helen Keller was born normal and had all of her faculties. At about the age of three, she was inflicted with a horrendous disease that took her sight and hearing. Helen became a vicious little animal, spoiled and incorrigible to an unbelievable degree. When she was given food that didn't suit her, she threw it on the person that brought it. She would throw herself on the floor, bang her head, kick her feet, and make her pitiful efforts to scream.

This is the scene into which Anne Sullivan came. The first day there, Helen Keller threw food on her. Anne looked at her and said, "Little girl, you can act as you will; you can treat me as you want. But when I look at you, I see not a little animal, not a blind, deaf-mute, but I look at you and see one of God's children. Because I see one of God's children, I know that there is a special purpose for you, and I'm going to love you so much that something is going to be done, and you are going to make your contribution."

Helen Keller influenced the lives of millions of people, but had there been no Anne Sullivan, there would have been no Helen Keller as we know her. You treat people exactly as you see them.

Once, as the story goes, a man was given the privilege of seeing both heaven and hell while he was still on earth. Satan spoke up and said, "Let me go first. Let me show him my place."

They went into hell and walked into a mammoth banquet hall. In this hall, there was the feast of the universe. Every conceivable kind of food, every fresh fruit, every fresh vegetable, all the pastries, all of the meats—everything that any human being could possibly desire.

But when the visitor looked into the eyes of the people who were seated there, he saw they were hollow. There was no music, no laughter, no happiness, and they looked as if they were starving to death.

Then the man was taken to heaven. He saw exactly the same scene, with exactly the same food, but this time people were laughing, singing, and having a good time.

The visitor said, "I'm puzzled. Will you explain what the difference is? They've got the same things to eat."

The guide said, "As you noticed, in both heaven and hell, each person had a four-foot-long fork and a four-foot-long knife strapped to each arm. In hell, they are trying to eat with forks and knives that are four feet long, and you just can't do it. But in heaven, they're feeding the person across from them."

You can get everything in life you want if you will just help enough other people get what they want. You see, you in fact do treat people exactly as you see those people. As Harvey Firestone observed, you get the best out of others when you give the best of yourself.

6

Sustaining Lifetime Love

For many years in our family, we had three daughters. Ten years later, like Abraham and Sarah, we were blessed in our old age with a little boy. But for many years, we had the three children.

When our third child was born, we knew that our middle child would be "different." We knew that because all of our friends and relatives had said, "The middle child is going to be different."

Remember, you treat people exactly as you see them. How many times did I contribute to the problem? I would say, "Why does Cindy have to cry all the time? Why does she whine so much? Why can't she be happy and excited like Suzan?"

As you know, kids want to cooperate, so Cindy cooperated. She became a whiner. Visitors didn't help. Somebody would come in the house, and the first thing they would do was walk over to my oldest daughter and say, "Oh, my! What a big girl you are. I bet you're a lot of help to mommy, aren't you?"

My eldest daughter would say, "Yes, ma'am, I try to be."

Then they'd go over to the baby, and they would ooh and aah: "Oh, what a cute little baby." But what about that oddball stuck off in the middle?

We knew Cindy was going to be different, and she didn't disappoint us a bit; she cooperated to the fullest. Then we learned that whatever you put in is going to come out. As you sow, so also shall you reap. So we started to use a different technique when somebody would come to see us. At that time, she was five years old, and her nickname was Tadpole. Somebody would come in, and I'd call her over to the side and introduce her to the visitor. I'd say, "I want to introduce you to the happiest little girl in this whole town. This is a little girl that everybody loves, because she's always smiling and having a good time. Aren't you, baby?"

She'd say, "Yes."

I'd say, "Tell them what your name is, baby."

She'd say, "Tadpole."

Then one day, when I asked her to tell her name to a visitor, she said, "Daddy, I've changed my name."

"What's your name now, baby?"

"I'm the happy Tadpole."

In less than a month, neighbors noticed the dramatic change that had taken place in Cindy. You see, Cindy didn't change until we had changed.

You treat people exactly as you see them, and the way you treat them has a bearing on what they do in life. Linda Isaac's a perfect example. Linda Isaac is a black girl. She's also a dwarf. When she was about four years old, experts did an evaluation on her and said, "Linda is mentally incompetent. She's never going to be able to learn anything." But she was a pleasant, happy little girl.

They put her in the first grade, and everybody said, "Linda can't learn anything, so don't waste too much time trying to teach her." So they passed her from the first grade to the second and on and on until she graduated from high school. Now we've got a dwarf functioning at the level of a first grader. What were her chances in life? Two: slim and none.

Linda's mother brought her to Dallas and moved her in with an older sister, who took her down to Goodwill Industries. Under the auspices of a federally funded program, they did some more testing on Linda and discovered that she might be able to learn. They gave her a simple little job, and it took her all morning to outgrow it. Then they gave her another little job, and it took her all day to outgrow that one. Then they gave her another one. A year after she finished high school, she was functioning at the level of a first grader. Because people were treating her like somebody who's capable of learning, she was able to learn.

Eventually, Linda got to the point where she could answer the telephone, check the payroll, and moved on to becoming a full-fledged secretary. It makes you wonder how many people we have in the game of life who are in exactly the same category: somebody had typed them early in their lives, said they could not learn, and proceeded to treat them that way all of the rest of their lives.

I used to have a college professor who, every time he started class, would pompously announce, "Nobody makes an A in my class. In fact, about 35 percent of you won't even pass."

Everybody around the school said, "That is a tough old buzzard," but when someone like that hides behind pompous academic baloney, you know what he's really saying? "I'm not bright enough to teach you enough to make an A. I don't know my subject well enough even to teach a third of you what the course is all about."

I was once in a department store in Columbia, South Carolina. There was a lady there, poorly dressed and, I gathered, with a very limited education. She became enthralled with a demonstration that was going on, and she forgot about her little girl, who was about five or six years old. The little girl drifted around five or six feet away from her. All of a sudden, the mother realized that her little girl was no longer close to her. When she did, she leaped like an animal and said, "You get over here. You know how scared you are of people."

I wonder what else that girl is going to be scared of for the rest of her life. I wonder how many times, she will be told, "If you don't do this, I'll let the policeman come get you."

There was an obscure college professor who had a wife, whom he loved very much, and she had a hearing problem. He went to work on designing a hearing aid, because he loved her and he wanted to be able to communicate with her. History tells us that he was never able to perfect the hearing aid, but in the process he came up with another invention, known as the telephone.

We treat people as we see them. I'm very much concerned about the way we deal with the ex-convict in America today. Society says that when a law is broken, punishment should be extracted. Sometimes it is, and sometimes it isn't, but let's assume that we do send a convict to prison because he's broken the law. At the end of the sentence, we say to him, "OK, you've paid your debt. Everything is even." But is it? Apparently not, because many times, when the ex-convict goes to a prospective employer and says, "I'm an ex-con," they don't hire him. If he does not tell them that he is an ex-con and they find out later, they fire him.

The net result is that ex-convicts end up frustrated and defeated. They say, "Society is still extracting its pound of flesh for what I've done. But I've got to have something to eat. Besides, it'll serve them right, because they've treated me wrong." With thinking like this, over 80 percent of ex-cons end up right back in prison.

We have an interesting concept of justice. Christ tells us the solution in Luke 17:3: "If thy brother trespass against thee, rebuke him; and if he repent, forgive him." Very simple.

Jesus Christ brought this point to a head in the story of the woman taken in the act of adultery. The Scribes and Pharisees were going to stone her, which was the law of the day. They brought her to Christ and said, "What should we do?" He stooped down and started writing on the ground. For a moment, he did not answer. They kept asking him, and he looked up and said, "He that is without sin among you, let him first cast a stone at her." Then he went back to writing in the sand. When he looked up, he discovered that no one was there. He said to the woman, "Where are your accusers?"

She said, "They're gone, Lord." As the Bible puts it in its beautiful simplicity, "They which heard it, being convicted by their own conscience, went out one by one" (John 8:1–11).

During World War II, a baker had a problem. He was buying butter from a farmer and he became convinced that the farmer was shortchanging him. He hauled the farmer into court and said, "This man is shortchanging me every day on my butter."

The judge said to the farmer, "What do you have to say about this to the baker?"

The farmer says, "I don't understand how I could possibly do that. I lost my one-pound weight, and every day when I weigh the butter, I do it with a loaf of bread, which I buy from the baker, which weighs a pound."

Most of us have a double set of standards, and we want to judge other people by an entirely different set from the one we use for ourselves. Yet we are in fact our brother's keeper.

I love the story of the old man who was playing the organ in a beautiful cathedral in Europe. He played skillfully and beautifully, but on this particular day, he was playing sad tunes, because today was his last day. He was being replaced by a young organist. As the sun was setting and the beautiful stained-glass windows reflected the light, the old man was almost angelic in appearance.

Toward the end of the day, a young man walked in the back door of the cathedral, and he stood there to listen to the old man play. The old man saw him, reached up, and switched off the organ. He put the key in his pocket and went to the back of the cathedral. The young man simply stuck his hand out and said, "Please, the key."

The old man gave the young man the key. The young man ran to the front of the cathedral and stood for an instant in front of the bench. Then he sat on the bench, inserted the key, and started to play. Although the old man had played beautifully, the young man played with sheer genius. The music filled the cathedral; it filled the town; it filled the countryside—music such as the world had never heard before.

This was the world's introduction to the music of Johann Sebastian Bach. With tears streaming down his cheeks, the old man said, "Suppose, just suppose, that I had not given the master the key."

I'd like to discuss one of the greatest mysteries that I've ever been confronted with. I have seen a businessman who is courteous to his secretary, thoughtful when the postman comes in, considerate to a deliveryman, and thoughtful even to a stranger, spending a lot of time giving them directions. Then his wife, the one he has sworn to love and cherish all his life, comes on the telephone with a simple question. He says, "Don't you know I don't like you to call me down here? I'm awfully busy. I'll get back to you as quickly as I can."

Occasionally I've seen this happen too. A husband will call his wife and say, "Honey, would you pick up my suit down at the cleaner's? I need to wear it this evening."

Even though she hasn't really been doing anything that morning, she says, "I'm too busy right now."

I'm going to talk about this other person that is so terribly important because I believe any man or any woman is more productive if they've got the unqualified support of their mate. I believe they do better work; I believe they can accomplish more. If you are privileged to have a happy marriage, you know exactly what I'm talking about. I don't hold myself up as a marital expert by any stretch of imagination, but God has blessed me for decades with a beautiful woman that's been mine all of these years. So it's from a happy experience that I do want to share some basic thoughts with you.

History has demonstrated that no society has ever survived after its family life deteriorated. Yet in our country, divorce rates are high and are expected to increase still more. I believe one major reason is that husbands and wives grow accustomed to having their mate around and assume that they always will be. Psychiatrist James Lieberman once estimated that the average couple who has been married over one year spends thirty-seven minutes a week talking to each other openly and without any other activity.

The second cause is our social environment. I believe that comedians today are creating a tremendous problem. Everywhere you go, some comedian is making fun, and ninety-nine times out of 100, it's of the wife or the mother-in-law. I've seen husbands laugh about the "old battle-ax," and everybody laughs along. Twenty minutes later, everybody's forgotten about it except the wife. She carries it for a year or even five or ten years. They say, "She doesn't really care." Don't you ever believe it. Not only does she care, but in one form or another, she is making him pay for it. In the process, of course, she makes herself pay too.

Another problem is the changing morality. Today people talk about wife swapping and living with somebody without being married. I've got to believe that this is a major problem. The people who believed that trial marriages would reduce the divorce rates are now forced to admit that they increase, not only the percentage of divorces, but the number of suicides among the people who are involved.

I believe the foundation for marriage, of course, is love. I believe John 3:16 describes love at its infinite best. I believe that if you'll read the thirteenth chapter of First Corinthians, you will further understand what love really is all about, but I want to discuss it just for a moment as it relates to our children.

Psychologists tell us that children are more secure knowing that mother and daddy love each other—even more secure than if they know that mother and daddy love them. If they know mother and daddy love each other, they know they're never going to have to choose which one they're going to live with. And they want the security of knowing that mother and dad are in fact going to be together.

I was going through some of my mail and came across a birthday card that I received a few years ago from my Happy Tadpole. At the bottom of it, she said, "Thank you, Daddy, for loving Mom so much." I tell you: it makes all the difference in the world.

Dr. George Crane, a psychologist from Chicago, says that even if you've fallen out of love with your mate, you can fall back in love. If you enthusiastically, positively reaffirm the love that you originally felt, even though it's been gone for a period of time, it will begin to grow again.

Let me share with you my first exposure to real love. It took place between a brother of mine and his wife. He's a preacher down in southern Alabama. His wife of thirty-three years had gone to Michigan City, Indiana, to be with their daughter at the birth of her first baby. She was gone ten days. When she came back, I was sitting out on the front porch, and my brother was in the kitchen. His son drove my brother's wife into the yard. As my brother heard the slamming of the car door, he rushed out to the front yard. His wife was out of the car. They embraced and cried like babies. Each one saying that never again would they ever let anything come between them, that never again would anything ever separate them, and that if there were other grandchildren, they would both be present for that occasion.

What a shame that this scene between this little country preacher and his helpmate could not have been captured on film and piped into every home in America! How beautiful it would have been to let everyone see what love is really all about—love that had been born in adolescence, nurtured in young adulthood, matured in middle age, and reached its zenith in the golden years of their life.

Real love is a growing and meaningful process that involves every emotion, problem, joy, and triumph known to man. It's more often hard than easy, more demanding than rewarding, and more confining than freeing; frequently, it involves more problems than pleasure.

Such was the case with Huey and Jewel Ziglar, my brother and his wife. They started on a shoestring and often reached what appeared to be the end of that shoestring. When it happened, and it often did, they simply tied a knot in the string and held on. He gave her his best, his all. He loved her, respected her, petted her, and courted her like the jewel she is. Five boys and a girl required lots of money, lots of time, and lots of loving discipline. But together, through their unshakable faith in Almighty God, they raised a beautiful family.

In the Ziglar household, I'm known as the word merchant. But when we gather together at brother Huey's with his family, and he starts talking about his dog, old Bullet, he has the children and the grandchildren in gales of laughter. You can sense the enormous amount of family love that prevails there.

That's what love is all about. By now, you must surely know that I'm one of those old-fashioned guys who believe in God and family and country, and I also believe that those vows "for better or worse" are not just words. These are opportunities to stay and grow together. Just as fine steel can be truly tempered only by heat and cold and highways can only be made safe by adding hills, valleys, and curves, so must marriage and love be built in the crucibles of trials and tribulations.

That's why it's so distressing to see young men and women flout the laws of God with trial marriages or calling it quits at the first straw in the windstorm before they've had time to know each other, much less love each other. They have no concept of what love between two responsible people is all about. They haven't learned to differentiate between love and sex. They don't realize when sex is a manifestation of love, it's truly beautiful and as God intended. When it is an expression of lust, it is animalistic and selfish.

Contrary to what the poets and TV writers say, love is not an instant emotion. Personally, I was attracted to my beautiful redhead the first time I ever saw her. I thought she was the sharpest gal going. I really thought I loved her when I'd known her just a brief period of time. At the end of the year, if you'd asked me if I loved her, I would have said yes. There was no doubt that I loved her after ten and fifteen and twenty years, but I did not really know what love was all about until I had been married to my wife for over twenty-five years.

That's partly why I think it's so sad that people start out in life with an objective of trying out a relationship to see if it works: "If it doesn't work, we'll simply get a divorce, because that is the easiest way out." They do not have that long-range objective.

Let's look at some ways to improve our marital relationships. To begin with, fellows, I think you ought to kiss your wife goodbye every day. And I'm not talking about a kiss or goodbye of the sort you would give to your sister. For your own good, you ought to kiss her goodbye. Some German insurance companies released a study saying that the man who kisses his wife goodbye every day has a life expectancy that's five years longer. Moreover, he will earn 20 to 35 percent more money and he will have 50 percent less time lost on the job. So to create a happy marriage, kiss your wife goodbye.

Next, forget the old garbage about the fact that marriage is a 50/50 proposition. It absolutely is not. It is a 100 percent/100 percent proposition. She deserves 100 percent of your interest. And girls, he deserves 100 percent of your interest. Start and end every day with that expression of love. Somebody asked, "When should you tell your wife or husband that you love them?" The obvious answer is, you tell your mate you love them before somebody else does.

You want to build a happy marriage? Let me use the best advice I can ever give you: go back to courting her exactly as you did before you met her. You remember how it was? You were so motivated, and you couldn't wait until the minute came when you would see her again. You'd go to a social event; some predatory male would make his approach, and you would tuck that little gal behind you and you would stick out your hand. During the course of the evening, people would think you were Siamese twins.

And you know how it was, girls. You would say to mom, "Mom, I met him today."

"Who is him?"

"Oh, mom, he's the most wonderful man. You'll just love him. He has the cutest ways." You would tell mom about this magnificent specimen of manhood.

Then one day, you got married. How many times have I heard a businessman say, "I'm running forty-five minutes late again, but she'll understand." Or the wife says, "It's hamburger again for the fourth night this week, but he'll understand." Obviously, somebody isn't understanding, because 48 percent of them are ending up in divorce.

What are we going to do about it? Many things. We've got to spend some quality time together. We've got to learn how to listen to what each other has to say—and I'm talking about the details. We've got to understand that neither the husband nor the wife should have to compete with the children for their mate's attention. I believe that two things are wrong: the mother who spends all of her time with a child and the mother who spends none of her time with the child. I think a good balance can be reached along the way.

I would hate for you to believe that my wife and I never had any disagreements, because we certainly do, but we never go to sleep with one. That's critically important, because if you go to sleep with a disagreement, it smolders, festers, and digs into the subconscious mind. We never go to sleep over our disagreements.

Love, if it's real, must be expressed; it must be shown. I think Shakespeare was right in saying that when they do not love, they do not show their love. I call that redhead when I'm away overnight and tell her I love her. The reason is not to educate her, because she already knows that, but I want to reinforce the idea. I want her to go to sleep every night knowing that that is a fact of life.

I also believe fervently that God's book says that I'm the head of my house, just as it says that God is the head of me, and he established the chain of command. I seldom if ever see a happy marriage in which the man did not act as a man. Now you must also read the rest of the scriptures: "So ought men to love their wives as their own bodies. He that loveth his wife loveth himself" (Ephesians 5:28). I'm not going to abuse my body, and I am not going to abuse my wife.

It's never a question of "I'm the boss, and therefore you're going to do it." But sometimes there are decisions that must be made after we have discussed them at length. If she thinks one thing and I think something else, I make the decision. I relieve her of that responsibility. She has the strength of knowing that I am going to assume that role.

I believe that if you will check the history of civilization, you're going to discover that the man is selected by God for that role. I also believe there was a specific reason God took the woman from man's side. He did not take her from a man's head, so that she could lord it over him, nor from his feet, so that he could trample her, but rather from his side, so they could go down life's highway together.

I believe there are certain responsibilities that men ought to have, and I believe there are certain responsibilities that women ought to have. Don't misunderstand: if my wife is sick, not only will I buy the groceries but I will cook the food, wash the dishes, mop the floors, and do anything else. But I also believe that a little boy needs to grow up seeing his father in an essentially masculine role. I believe that little girls need to grow up seeing their mothers in an essentially feminine role. If from the very beginning they can tell that there is a distinct difference between the male and the female, many of the difficulties that we're experiencing in our land today will largely be solved.

I believe we are to look to Ephesians 4:32 as a guiding light every day: "Be ye kind one to another, tenderhearted, forgiving one another." I think it's a foundation for marriage. I was also pleased to discover recently that families who prayed together daily have considerably less than a 3 percent rate of divorce.

Here are some more specifics. I think the husband needs to share with the wife the details of what's going on with him. I believe that the husband needs to write his wife little love letters every once in a while. I also think he ought to call her once or twice a week and just say, "Honey, I had a minute. Wanted to call you and let you know that I love you."

Girls, if you send your husband off to work every day with a cold lunch, I believe that you ought to put a warm note in it to let him know you will be glad when he gets home. When he gets home, I don't believe you ought to be in the back of the house, saying, "Is that you, honey?" I think you ought to be at the front door, letting him know that you know it's honey and that you are delighted to see him.

Sometimes my wife writes little signs for me and hangs them up. I pull in my garage sometimes, and a sign will say, "Welcome home, honey." It must have taken her all of two minutes to have painted that sign, but I get excited when I see it. Once in a while, I'll see a little note on the bottom that says, "Baked sweet potatoes for supper tonight." Now you're not going to believe this, but there are some people who don't like baked sweet potatoes mashed up with lots of good butter, and my redhead is one of them. When she has baked sweet potatoes for supper, it says to me, "Honey, I was thinking about you when I bought them. I was thinking about you when I put them in the cabinet. I was thinking about you when I put them in the oven. I was thinking about you when I wrote this little note."

The applause of a single human being is of great consequence. It's especially significant when it's from the person who has sworn to love the other. I don't know why, but many times people miss the chance to tell someone, "I love my wife," or "I love my husband." Many times, when I have heard somebody say something nice about a woman's husband, she'll comment, "Oh, he's all right." Or somebody will say something nice about the wife to the husband, and he'll say, "Well, yeah, she is a good girl." Why not say, "That's the reason I fell heavily and deeply in love with that girl," or "That's why I love my husband so much—because he is that kind of a guy"? If you think this is mushy, let me simply say this: until you try it and find out what excitement in love and marriage really are, don't you dare be critical of it.

It makes all the difference in the world; it'll turn a marriage around.

One morning a man in Atlanta called me and woke me up. He said, "Zig, got a problem. My wife is leaving me. She wants a divorce. I don't want her to have it. Can you help me?"

"Let me send you some thoughts," I said, and I sent them to him.

About a week later, the man woke me up again, and this time he got his wife on the telephone. She said, "Zig, we are so excited and happy to be together. What you're saying actually works. But we took you seriously for a reason you never guessed.

"We were at a convention at the Fairmont Hotel in Dallas, and you and your wife walked in to have dinner that evening. You didn't know we were there. You never saw us. But when we saw the two of you together, holding hands, thoroughly enjoying each other as man and wife, oblivious to anything else that was going on around you, we knew that what you were saying was completely from the heart."

I think the greatest institution in the world is a magnificent marriage, where husbands and wives love each other and are considerate, thoughtful, and helpful to each other.

Let me give you two last thoughts for wives. If your husband brings you something, make it easy for him to bring you something else. Many a husband brings a wife a present, and she says things like, "Why did you buy that color? You know I don't look good in orange." Or, "Honey, you know I wear a small, and that's the medium large. Couldn't you have done better than that?" Or, "You know I'm on a diet, and I can't eat any candy." "Why did you spend $20 for roses? You know I needed that new blouse."

In all my years of marriage, I have never made a mistake in bringing my wife anything. Whatever I bring her is always at the top of her shopping list. It's exactly what she wanted. It's the perfect size, the perfect color, in perfect taste. Now I will be the first to confess that a lot of times I never see it again, and something else shows up in its place. But I'll tell you, she made me feel as if the smartest thing I had ever done was to pick out that gift. And you know what? I am motivated to buy something else. It's easy, and it's fun under circumstances like that.

Girls, brag about your husband. If your man is out doing the best he can, he desperately wants you to brag about him and be proud of him. Sometimes when I give a presentation, people come up afterward and say, "That was fantastic." As much as I treasure them, these comments would be meaningless until my wife came to me and said, "Honey, you done good!"

Brag on the man; make him feel proud of what he's doing. Brag on the girls, fellows; make them feel proud of what they are doing. Marriage and the family are the foundation of our country. It's critically important that you preserve yours. And I promise you that if you do these things, you're going to have more fun than you ever dreamed possible. It's a fantastic way to live.

Let me conclude by reiterating the purposes of the previous two chapters:
1. To clarify the way you should see other people.
2. To sell the concept that you treat other people as you see them.
3. To establish that you can get everything in life you want if you will just help enough other people get what they want.
4. To identify genuine love and give specific suggestions on how to court after you're married.

At this point, you can evaluate whether or not you have accomplished your objectives.

7

The Power of Goals

Now we get into one of the most exciting phases of this book: goals. Here we have six clear purposes:

1. To sell you on the importance of goals in your personal and professional life.
2. To explain why most people never set goals.
3. To identify the kinds of goals you should have and their characteristics.
4. To elaborate on the characteristics of goals.
5. To spell out in specific detail how to set your goals.
6. To give detailed procedures for reaching your goals.

I'm confident that as we go through this process, you will be able to identify these purposes. I believe that if you define what your objectives are, you can reach them. Most people, however, never define what they want in life. Then they wonder why they don't get everything that they allegedly dream about wanting.

This reminds me of the story about an old boy down home. His wife sent him out to buy ham. When he got home with it, she said, "You didn't have the end of the ham cut off."

"Why do you want the end of the ham cut off?"

"We always cut the end of the ham off."

"Why?"

"We cut the end of the ham off because my mama cut the end of the ham off."

So they went to the kitchen, where her mama was, and asked, "Mama, how come you cut the end of the ham off?"

Mama said, "I always cut the end of the ham off because my momma cut the end of the ham off."

"We're going to solve this three-generation mystery in a hurry," said the old boy. "Let's call grandma long-distance. Let's find out why she cut the end of the ham off."

So they called grandma long-distance and asked her, "Grandma, how come you cut the end of the ham off?"

Grandma said, "I cut the end of the ham off because my roaster was too small."

Now, you see, Grandma had a reason. But what about you? Have you got a reason, or do you just follow? Do you do things just because that's always the way it's been done?

This is an absolute fact: when they move sheep from one pasture to another, if they put a little bar up as they go from one pasture to another, the first sheep will jump the bar, the second sheep will jump the bar, and the third sheep will jump the bar. Then they move the bar, but every sheep from there on in will keep jumping a bar that's not there.

A lot of people jump bars that are not there. A lot of people climb a lot of mountains that don't exist. They have difficulties simply because they never define what their objectives really are.

The name Howard Hill might not ring a bell with you, but he was a good Alabama boy, and he also was the greatest archer that ever lived. Howard Hill won 296 consecutive archery tournaments. He was never beaten in competition. He won six national championships before he was forced into retirement. He was forced to retire because when he entered the tournament, all other archers automatically withdrew, knowing he would win.

When I was a youngster, I watched newsreels and saw Howard Hill hit a bull's-eye dead center at fifty feet. It wasn't a fraction of an inch off. He then would take the next arrow and he would split the first arrow. An amazing demonstration of skill.

Now I could take you—and I don't care who you are or where you live—spend twenty minutes teaching you about archery. Even though you've never had any previous experience, I can guarantee you that I will have you hitting the bull's-eye more consistently than Howard Hill—provided that you blindfold Howard Hill.

You might say, "That's silly. Obviously, I could hit a bull's-eye better than a man who's blindfolded. How in the world could a man hit a target that he could not see?"

That's a legitimate question. Here's another one that I think is equally legitimate: how can you hit a target that you don't have? Have you got one? Oh, someday you're going to have a big home, a big car, and a big bank account, and someday you are going to accomplish this, that, and the other.

Those are what we call *wandering generalities*.

You'll never make it big in the ball game of life as a wandering generality. You've got to be a meaningful specific.

I love the story of Jean-Henri Fabre, a French naturalist who used some processionary caterpillars in an intriguing experiment. Now they're called *processionary* because one caterpillar follows the other in a procession—blindly, without question, without hesitation; they just follow the one in front.

Fabre took some of these caterpillars and lined them around a flowerpot until they formed a complete circle, and they were moving in this complete circle. He put some pine needles—these caterpillars' favorite food—in the center. The caterpillars went round and round for seven full days and seven full nights until they dropped dead of starvation and exhaustion. With their favorite food less than three inches away, they starved to death.

We see this right here in America, in the richest land in the world. With an abundance of wealth at their fingertips, these people are failing to succeed because they behave like processionary caterpillars. They confuse activity with accomplishment. There's a vast difference.

That's one reason you could go in any city in the U.S.A., stop 100 young men on the street and ask them, "What are you doing that will guarantee your failure in life?"

I can guarantee that all 100 would look at you and say, "What do you mean what am I doing to guarantee my failure? I am in fact working for success."

If they are, something is wrong, because if you follow all 100 of them starting at age twenty-five and follow them until they're sixty-five, only five of those 100 will have made it. Only five will be successful financially. Only one of them will be wealthy.

That's in America, a land that's so unique that a few years ago, I saw where a man had been released from the federal penitentiary in Atlanta, and he had accumulated a small fortune in prison, running a little tailor shop there. This land is so unique that it lets even a prisoner who uses his imagination and ingenuity create wealth within a prison. Yet only a small fraction of the free people in America accomplish their objectives.

Why is this? Once I was flying over Niagara Falls, and the captain of the aircraft came over the intercom and said, "Ladies and gentlemen, those of you who have never seen the falls from the air should look to the left-hand side of the aircraft, because it is a magnificent sight." We were ten miles above the falls, but I could still see the spray coming up. Three million gallons a minute were falling 180 feet, and even from that great distance, you could feel the awesome power of Niagara.

As I looked at the view, my mind turned backwards through the thousands of years that trillions of gallons of water had fallen over Niagara Falls and dissipated in the distance. Then one day a man came along with a plan. He looked at the falling water and the enormous power that it was generating and said, "If we were to put some wheels there, and catch just a small portion of the water as it falls and get it to turn in those wheels, we could generate electricity. We could build homes, schools, factories, and hospitals, and we could create industry and wealth." And the man did exactly that.

Even though these turbines catch only a small fraction of the water, they've generated trillions of kilowatt-hours of electricity. They have educated children. They have healed illnesses. They have created prosperity and wealth. They have built buildings, automobiles, schools, and factories and contributed tremendously to the economic value and growth of that entire area. It happened because a man came along who had a plan.

You've got to have a goal. Actually, we have many goals: family goals, mental goals, physical goals, social goals, spiritual goals, and, yes, financial goals. Many years ago, J. C. Penney said, "Give me a stock clerk with a goal, and I'll give you a man who'll make history, but give me a man without a goal, and I'll give you a stock clerk."

Imagine somebody going up to the chairman of the board for General Motors and asking, "How did you happen to become chairman of the board? How did you get all the way to the top?" Imagine him replying, "I just started showing up for work every day, and they promoted me. I showed up again, and they promoted me again. I kept showing up, they kept promoting me, and here I am, chairman of the board."

You'll say, "That's silly," and of course it is. You've got to have a goal, because it's just as difficult to reach a destination that you don't have as it is to come back from a place you've never been. That's awfully tough.

Charles Schwab, who headed Bethlehem Steel for Andrew Carnegie in the early twentieth century, was adept at getting other people to utilize their enormous amount of ability. As a matter of fact, under Carnegie's jurisdiction, he created thirty-four millionaires, during the days when a millionaire was somebody who had an awful lot of money.

Charles Schwab was concerned about one of his steel mills. They were dragging their feet. He walked into the mill one day and walked straight to the foreman. It was about quitting time for that shift, and Schwab asked, "I want to find out what the difficulty is here. Why is this mill not producing more?"

The foreman said, "Mr. Schwab, I don't know. I've tried everything I know. I've tried to enthuse them. I've tried to motivate them. I pat some of them on the back, some of them high, some of them low. I do everything I can to get them to produce, but nothing seems to happen."

Schwab said, "How many heats have you completed today?"

The foreman said, "Six."

Schwab took a big piece of chalk and wrote a huge six at the entrance to the mill. As the shift was changing, the night foreman saw the six and said, "What is that?" He was told that was the number of heats the day shift had finished that day.

I don't think I need to tell you, but that night the night shift produced seven heats. The next morning, as they were going off shift, they wrote a monstrous seven right at the entrance. As he was coming back on, the day foreman did not need to be told what that seven represented. He called a meeting and explained what had happened overnight. The same men who the day before had just produced six heats now, in the same plant under the same circumstances, produced ten.

Three factors were involved. First of all, these men had a goal: they had a definite goal of beating the team before them. They had seen the cross-bar, and they were determined to go beyond it. Second, they had their own personal pride at stake. They wanted to be part of a winning team. Third was team spirit. With all of these things involved, their production went up immediately.

Let's play a little game. Let's pretend that tomorrow morning you get a phone call, and the voice at the other end says, "Sally, I've got fantastic news for you. You and your husband have just been invited to attend a three-day retreat at one of the most beautiful resorts in all of America.

It's in an indescribably beautiful setting. You're going to be staying in one of the most beautiful condominiums you have ever seen. You're going to be overlooking a lake. You're going to have a big, magnificent boat. Everything is going to be at your beck and call. You and your husband are going to be wined and dined. You're going to be given every courtesy. You're going to have the run of the place. You're going to be the queen of the walk. You're getting this little trip simply because we have room for two more, and it won't cost us anything. I know you'll enjoy the trip, so we're going to invite you and your husband to go. They're going to pick you up at your hometown airport in the corporate jet. All I want to know is, can you be ready to go tomorrow morning at 8:30?"

If you were to get that call, would you be ready to go tomorrow morning at 8:30? I know what would go through your mind immediately: "Oh, boy, will I ever be ready." But once you hung up, you would start thinking, "I've got to do this, and I've got to do that." You and your husband would have a little council of war, and you'd start saying, "I'll tell you what. I can get this done, and you take care of that one." You would put down exactly what you had to do, and you would divide the chores. Do you think that during the next twenty-four hours, you'd be able to do more than you normally do in four or five days?

In your mind, you'd say, "Yessiree, I'd be ready to go." Then you would identify all of the things that you had to do before you could go. You would have set a goal, identified the obstacles that stand between you and the goal, and determined the way to overcome them. That's really what goal setting is all about, isn't it?

We're going to have a Super Bowl next January. I don't know who's going to be in it, but I do know what will happen during the two weeks beforehand: the coaching staff of the two teams involved will spend something over 500 hours in setting the game plan for that one game. Oh, it's an important game, there's no doubt about it. But did you know that many people spend more time planning a vacation or an evening out than on planning their entire lives?

Why don't people have goals? Everybody talks about it; everybody agrees that it's important. Everybody agrees that you should have them, yet most people don't. Many times I've talked to people about goals, and the answer I get is, "I've got my goals, but I'm not going to tell you what they are, because I hate these smart alecks who are always talking about what they're going to do and then don't do it. As soon as I get there, I'll tell you what my goal was."

You know what they're really saying? "Look, friend, I'm scared to death I'm not going to make it, and I don't want to be wrong at the top of my voice." So they never set their goals. When those people get to be old, they're going to be looking over the fence, watching somebody else gather all the apples.

Some people say, "I've never set goals because nobody ever told me exactly how to set them, or they've never really convinced me that I ought to set those goals now." Others are going to set them as soon as they get around to it. This is why I'm including this information in this book.

Let's look at some of the characteristics of goals. First of all, they've got to be big. A goal has got to be big in order to create excitement, because unless you're excited about what you're doing, unless you're moving and motivated, unless you're determined to utilize the enormous potential that's inside of you, a goal is going to be meaningless. That's often why a good tennis player is beaten by a mediocre one: the good player did not feel challenged enough. Similarly, a good football team is often beaten by a mediocre team because they did not feel sufficiently challenged, and they became overconfident. You've got to have a big goal to force you to reach down and use everything that's inside of you.

When I was a boy down in Yazoo City, the store where I worked was next to a coffee and peanut shop. There's a man who ran the shop named Uncle Joe: that's all anybody ever knew him by. Uncle Joe used to roast the coffee and the peanuts, and when he was roasting, he gathered a crowd from miles around. It was a tantalizing odor.

I used to watch Uncle Joe as he finished roasting those peanuts. He would put the peanuts in a box, then he would take them from the box and fill the little bags. I sold those peanuts; they cost a nickel in those days. When he had finished filling a bag, he would reach in and take two peanuts out and put them into a separate little box. By the time he got through with the big box, he had a little box full of peanuts. Those were his bonuses, and he would fill the other bags from his little bonus box.

Uncle Joe was born a poor man, lived all of his life as a poor man, and died a poor man. He dealt with peanuts all of his life, but peanuts were not his problem. During World War II, when I was transferred to the naval program at the University of South Carolina in Columbia, as I rode into town, I saw a big sign that said, "Cromer's P-Nuts: Guaranteed Worst in Town."

I was intrigued with that sign, so I inquired about this man. Somebody said, "Oh, yes, that's Mr. Cromer, and he does a fantastic job with peanuts." A few years before, he had started in a little stall down on Market Street in Columbia, and he put up a sign: "Cromer's P-Nuts, Guaranteed Worst in Town." People looked at him and smiled, but they bought the peanuts.

Later on, Cromer put up bigger signs and started putting his motto on his bags of peanuts: "Cromer's P-Nuts: Guaranteed Worst in Town." People giggled, but they bought the peanuts. A little bit later, he got the franchise from the state fair and for the football and basketball games. Pretty soon, he had expanded all over the state. He had hundreds of boys out selling his peanuts, and he became a wealthy man.

Now these two men sold the same product under essentially the same circumstances. But one looked at it and saw it as simply a two-peanut operation, and the other one looked at it, used the multiplication scale, and saw a tremendous opportunity.

You see, it's not what it is, it's the way you see it that's important, whether you're the butcher, the baker, or the candlestick maker, or whether you're a salesman, doctor, service station owner, or minister. Some of your colleagues are faring extremely well doing exactly the same thing you're doing, and some of them are not doing well at all. It's not the job or the profession that is the opportunity; it's the way the individual sees that job or profession. You've got to have a big goal. Look at the leadership, at the people who are doing the top jobs in your profession. Use them as your models, and you can succeed.

Not only does a goal have to be big, it's got to be long-range, because we're going to have some frustrations in everyday activities. People may disappoint us. There are going to be activities that we're not going to approve of. There will be incidents that would discourage us if we did not have long-range goals.

The rule is very simple: you go as far as you can see, and when you get there, you'll always be able to see further.

Let's say I'm taking a flight to Memphis. When that aircraft takes off, we will be headed directly for Memphis. We'll fly to Memphis for about fifteen minutes, and then we will no longer be going to Memphis, because the direction and velocity of the wind will change, and we're going to be blown slightly off course. So the captain of the aircraft will turn the aircraft around and go back to the point of origin, right? Wrong. He's going to make a slight adjustment, and when he does, he'll be going back to Memphis again.

Why will the captain make that slight adjustment? First, because he knows exactly where he is going. He has a specific destination. If he just decided to get up in the air and say, "I think I'll take these folks for a little ride," he wouldn't know when he'd gotten off course. If you don't have a destination, how can you know when you're off course?

Most people are in fact wandering generalities. They show up for work every day and then avoid it. They do a lot of things, but they've never clearly spelled out exactly what they want in life.

If you don't have a long-range goal, when you think you deserve a promotion or you think something good is going to happen to you but you don't quite make it, many times that short-range frustration will destroy you.

My world has been the world of selling for an awfully long time. I've seen many people who would build an organization, build for the future, and build their own security. They would have an objective, but it would not be clearly defined; it would not be spelled out clearly enough. Frequently they'd get close: they would only need one or two more recruits or a certain volume of business in order to get a promotion; then the very people they knew were going to put them over the top quit on them.

What happens? About that time, "friends and relatives" enter the picture. A next-door neighbor says, "Well, Sally, I tried to tell you: everything that glitters is not gold. Just because somebody else did it does not necessarily mean that you can. Now I'm going to suggest this, Sally, for your own good: why don't you get a job?" If you don't have a clearly defined long-range objective, then you will react to disappointment and become susceptible to the influence of other people.

Yes, the rule is very simple: you've got to have a big, long-range goal, and it must be very specific. It also has to be something that you work on daily. We can romance long-range goals and get the stars in our eyes. We dream the big dream, and we see the big vision up there, all sweetness and light. But what you do every day will determine whether or not you reach your big, long-range goal.

Charlie Cullen, who was one of my favorites before his death, expressed it magnificently when he said, "The opportunity for greatness does not come cascading down like a torrential Niagara Falls. It comes slowly, one drop at a time."

It's what you do every day. It's the husbands and wives who demonstrate their love and affection daily that build a marriage that is going to endure. It's the mother who makes those daily deposits of love and discipline in her children that determines what they're going to be able to do in their lives. The weight lifter who wants to lift a lot of weight has got to start slowly and develop a muscle here and there on an everyday basis. What we do every day, our daily objectives, are the best indicators and the best builders of character. This is where our dedication, discipline, and determination enter the picture. This is what takes the glamour out and gets right down to the nitty-gritty.

Goals must be specific for a very simple reason: You can take the hot-test day the world has ever seen and take the most powerful magnifying glass that you can buy. You can hold that glass over a pile of newspaper clippings, but you will never start a fire if you keep the glass moving. Yet the instant you hold the glass still, you harness the power of the universe, multiply it through the glass, and boom! You've got a rip-roaring fire.

Goals can also be negative, so let's look at the three conditions under which a goal can be negative. First of all, if you don't accept the idea that you and you alone must be the architect of accomplishment, if you think luck is going to determine whether you get there or not, you've got a negative goal.

A goal can also be negative if it's not *your* goal. You cannot reach some-body else's objective. You must have your own clearly defined objectives.

Furthermore, a goal can be negative if it's unrealistically big. I know I'm going to have to walk a pretty thin line here, because I've been talking about big goals, but a goal can be too big.

Once I was speaking to a sales organization in Detroit. When I finished, a young man in his early twenties came up to me, and he was motivated to the point of being almost incoherent. He said, "Mr. Ziglar," he said, "you have done something for me today that's absolutely incredible. You have really made me a lot of money today."

"Well, friend," I said, "why don't you tell me about it?" although I couldn't have stopped him if my life depended on it.

He said, "You've made me $1 million this year."

Now I've got a problem, haven't I? Here's a man so excited that he can't breathe, yet he is saying he is going to make $1 million this year. I said, "I just hope you'll share it with me when you get it."

The young man was somewhat put out with me for even having the audacity to cast a doubt upon his ability to earn $1 million.

Now what do I do? Do I take a chance on destroying that initial enthu-siasm by saying that his goal is too big? Or do I let him go out, get his teeth kicked in, and then have him want to step off the world and let it go on without him?

I decided that I owed it to the young man to reason with him for a few moments. I looked at him. He was about twenty-four years old. Judging by the way he was dressed, I don't believe that if it cost four bits to go around the world, the kid could have gotten out of sight. In other words, I think he was broke.

The young man acknowledged to me that he did not have the $2,000 necessary to buy the inventory to get started. Here he is, twenty-four years old. In twenty-four years, he's been unable to save $2,000, but during the next twelve months, he is going to accumulate $1 million. That's $20,000 a week. Now just to be fair, let's assume that it takes him six weeks to get the $2,000. He's already $120,000 behind. Let's say it takes him another four weeks to get started. That's another $80,000; now he's $200,000 behind on his objective. By now, his friends and relatives would have laughed him out of the ballpark, wouldn't they?

I think his goal was too big. I'm not saying it was impossible, because sometimes people amaze me with what they can do. I never use the word *impossible*, but I do believe his goal was unrealistic and improbable.

I was on a local talk show once, and the interviewer said, "I take it that because of your positive thinking, you believe you can just do anything."

"No, ma'am," I said, "I sure don't believe that."

She looked a little bit surprised. She said, "Would you explain?"

"I'd be glad to," I said. "However positive I get, however hard I train, and however diligently I seek instruction, I don't believe that if you were to put me in the ring with Muhammad Ali, I could whip him. That goal is out of my area of interest. I'm too old, I'm too slow, and I'm too scared. I just don't think I'd have a chance."

I don't think positive thinking would enable me to accomplish that objective. I think that goal—and it is an exaggerated one, obviously—is too big. I believe the young man had a goal that was too big.

Incidentally, some people will deliberately set a goal that's too big. Many times, they will set a goal knowing that it's impossible for them to reach, because they're not seeking admiration for accomplishment; they're seeking sympathy. When they don't reach the goal, their friends are inclined to say, "That was too ambitious," or "It was too big."

Now that I've said this, let's find out exactly what we must do to reach our goals. First of all, you have to find out where you are. You see, most people never realize exactly where they are.

Years ago, when I was in the cookware business, I had a young salesman in my office. It was early in December. "What are your plans for next year?" I asked.

"I'll tell you one thing: I'm going to sell more next year than I sold this year."

"That's fantastic. How much did you sell this year?"

With a big old smile on his face, he said, "I don't know exactly, but I guarantee you, I'll sell more next year."

That's interesting, isn't it? He didn't know where he was and had no idea where he had been, but with the confidence that generally goes with ignorance, he said, "I know where I am going."

Before you laugh too loud and long, let me ask you: Do you know where you are? Do you know where you've been? If you can't answer these two questions, how can you determine where you're going? I don't believe that you can.

I challenged the young man to become an immortal in the cookware business.

He said, "How do I do that?"

"It's easy. You just break the all-time company record."

He was drinking a cup of coffee at the time, and I thought he was going to spill it all over everything. "You know I could never do that," he said.

"What do you mean you can never do it?"

"Not only could I not do it, but no man will ever break that record."

"What are you talking about?"

"The record's not honest. The guy that set the record had his son-in-law working for him, and the son-in-law sold as much as he did." You see the young man's loser's limp: the record was not honest.

"I believe the record is honest," I said. "I believe you can break it. All you've got to do is take the best week you've ever had, multiply it by fifty, and there's your record."

He grinned and said, "That's easy for you to say, but it's tough for me to do."

"Not only is it tough, it's impossible if you really don't believe that you can, because you are going to accomplish whatever you deeply believe you can."

He said, "I'll think about it." I was glad that he did, because a goal that's lightly set is also going to be lightly broken.

The telephone wires must have been burning up with excitement on December 26, when I got a phone call from Augusta, Georgia, to my home in Columbia, South Carolina. The young man called me and said, "Since our conversation, I have kept exact records. I know exactly how much business I get every time I knock on a door. I know how much business I get every time I make a phone call, every time I open my briefcase, every time I put on a demonstration. I know how much I sell every week, every day. I can even tell you how much business I sell every single hour that I work. I'm going to break that record."

"Oh, no, you're not going to break the record. I'd say you just broke it."

Let me tell you why I said that. He didn't use the word *if* anywhere in the conversation. If you take the two center letters out of the word *life*, you'll find that they are *if*. Half of life itself is *if*, and he didn't fall back on a single one. He didn't say, "I'll break the record *if* I don't wreck my car," or "I'll break that record *if* there are no deaths in my family" (and he buried two loved ones, including a brother). Nor did he say, "I'll break the record *if* I don't lose my voice." (In December, with the goal so close he could smell it and feel it and touch it, he completely lost his voice. For twenty-two agonizing days, he could not even whisper.) He simply said, "I'll break the record," period.

The most the young man had ever sold in a single year was $34,000, and that was not a bad job in itself back in those years. But the next year, selling the same product in the same area to the same people, at the same price, under the same economic conditions, he delivered and paid for over $104,000 worth of cookware: over three times as much.

I tell this story because it illustrates all the characteristics of goal setting and goal reaching. Number one, that was his goal. Nobody else set it for him. He wanted to do it. Number two, he found out where he was. He kept records. He knew exactly how much business he got when he made a sales call. Many times, I'll ask members of a sales organization, "How much do you sell every time you make a sales call?" They give me company averages, not what they're doing. But it's *your* average that's important, and this young man was talking about his own average: he found out exactly where he was.

The third thing about that young man's goal was that it was very specific. Fourth, it was a big goal, but not an impossible or irresponsible one. He had measured what he was capable of doing based on his past performance. Furthermore, it was a long-range goal—for one year—but he broke it into segments on a daily basis, and he was prepared mentally to discipline himself. Finally, he was confident that he was going to reach that particular goal.

When I started writing this book, I put some strong words in it: "You can go where you want to go; you can do what you want to do; you can be as you want to be." As I read those words, I said, "Zig, that's pretty good."

There's nothing wrong with talking to yourself and nothing wrong even with answering. But I found myself saying, "Huh?" to the answer, and I knew I was in trouble, because I had written, "You can be as you want to be." I had to hold those words a long way off, because I had a forty-one-inch waistline, and I weighed 202 pounds. The thought occurred to me that one of these days, I might run into somebody who had read the book and was going to say, "Zig, do you believe everything you wrote in that book?"

I was going to say, "Yeah."

"What about the part that says, 'You can be as you want to be?' Are you the way you want to be?"

Then I was going to say, "We authors have to take a little literary license every once in a while; you understand."

"In other words, Ziglar, I understand you're a liar."

"Man, don't call me a liar. Those are hard words."

"Well, you're a hypocrite, then."

"Don't call me a hypocrite."

As I was writing those words and looking at my forty-one-inch waistline, I said, "Zig, either you're going to have to take the words out of the book or you're going to have to do something about you."

The straw that broke the camel's back: my redhead kept telling me to hold my stomach in, and I already was. So I knew I had to do something. I went down to Cooper Clinic in Dallas. Its founder, Kenneth Cooper, wrote the book *Aerobics*, and when you see people out jogging, you can rest assured he had something to do with it.

I went down for the examination: five hours. The first thing they did was to take two quarts of my blood. At least it looked like two quarts. They just kept filling those little vials. I thought they were starting a blood bank right then and there. Then they dunked me in a tank of water three times to find my percentage of body fat. They told me I was 23.9 percent pure lard. Then they put me on a treadmill. The number of minutes you can walk determines your physical condition. I was somewhat chagrined to discover that I could only go four seconds.

When it was all over, the young examining physician, Dr. Martin, called me in. Of course he was skinny; he ran the Boston Marathon and all those good things. He smiled and said, "Mr. Ziglar," he said, "you're going to be very pleased to know that our calculations show that you are not overweight. However, you are exactly five and a half inches too short."

"Well, Doc, that's pretty bad."

"No, actually you're in remarkably good physical condition for a sixty-six-year-old."

"Doc, I'm forty-six."

"You're in awful shape. If you were a building, I'd condemn you."

"Well, Doc, what I can do?"

He whipped out a thick stack of papers and started telling me what I could do. By the time he got through, I was like the little boy that asked his daddy a question. His daddy said, "Why don't you ask your mother?" The little boy said, "I didn't want to know that much about it."

After the doctor had told me that much about it and I got home, my redhead said, "I suppose you're going to be out running all over the place now."

"Yes."

"If I'm going to have a forty-six-year-old fat boy running all over the place, I'm going to get you looking just as good as I can." She went down to the store and bought me some fancy running clothes.

When I was in the doctor's office, I did something that's kind of ugly: I tore a page out of a magazine. It was an advertisement for Jockey shorts. Now the ads don't show Jockey shorts on fat boys. I put up that picture of the fellow in the Jockey shorts in my bathroom, and I said, "Now that's it. That's the way I'm going to look one of these days. There's my hero."

The next morning, the alarm clock sounded and I hopped out of bed, slipped on that fancy running outfit, hit that front door, and ran a block. The next day, I did a whole lot better: I ran a block and a mailbox. The next day, it was a block and two mailboxes, then a block and three mailboxes. Then one day, I ran all the way around the block. I came back in, woke the whole family up, and I said, "Guess what Dad has done." Another day, I ran a half a mile, then one day I ran a mile, then a mile and a half, then two miles.

One day, I started doing sit-ups. At first, only eight, then ten, then twenty, then forty, then eighty, then 120. I started doing pushups: only six the first day, then eight, then ten, then twenty, then thirty, then forty. Today I do the GI pushup: you push up and clap your hands while you're in the air. My weight started coming down from 202 to 200, 190, 180, 170, and 165. My waistline dropped all the way from forty-one inches to thirty-four. Ten months before the book went to the publisher, I had already written that I weighed 165 pounds and had a thirty-four-inch waistline. To the ounce and to the day and to the inch, I was on target.

I give you all these details because you can take these identical principles and apply them to your own life. Whatever your goal is, you identify the principles and lay out your objectives. This is the way that you will be able to set and reach them.

I will say two or three things about dieting. First, make certain that you're the one who's interested in losing weight and nobody else has talked you into it. Second, do not get on a roller-coaster diet. One reason is psychological: if you lose twenty pounds and gain back thirty, you are worse off than if you had never lost any weight at all, because you've tried something and failed; now you've got another failure that you've got to overcome. The other reason is physiological. When you lose weight, you don't lose cells: the cells simply shrink. But when you gain weight, you gain cells. Therefore every time you go on a diet, it gets more and more difficult.

Dieting is not something that you play with. If you want to lose weight, go on a common-sense diet after you have had a thorough physical examination and you have completely determined that that's what you want to do.

Get an examination from a skinny doctor. If he is not skinny, he cannot give you everything you need, including the psychological reinforcement at the time you're going to need it. If he's overweight, he does not totally believe in what he's telling you to do.

Furthermore, if your doctor starts to give you a prescription for pills, don't walk out on him; run out. You didn't get overweight taking pills; you're not going to get underweight taking pills. Besides, if pills worked, there'd be no such thing as a fat doctor.

Finally, if the doctor tells you what you can't eat, swap doctors. If you're like 99.9 percent of all the Americans I've ever met, you are too ornery and obstinate and stubborn, and you don't want people telling you what you can't have. I don't have any earthly idea what I can't eat. Why should I clutter my mind with a bunch of stuff I can't even have? If you ask me what I *can* eat, then I'll tell you exactly: I can eat roast, steak, chicken, fish, vegetables, and salad. I don't want all this negativism going into my mind about what I can't have. We live in too negative a world as it is.

Let me now tell you about my diet insofar as goal setting was involved. First of all, it was my goal, and my credibility was at stake. Second, it was a very specific goal: 37 pounds is about as specific as you can get. Third, it was a big goal: that is a lot of weight. Fourth, I had broken it down into objectives. I knew my book was going to the publisher 10 months later. I looked at 37 and divided it by 10. That came out 3.7, and I knew that I could lose 3.7 pounds a month. That's not an insurmountable obstacle. This is very important: you've got to have the right mental attitude, knowing that you can accomplish your objective, or else you're going to have extreme difficulty in getting there. Finally, I put the goal on a daily basis. I divided the 3.7 by 30. I found out that all I had to do was lose 1.9 ounces a day, and I would lose 37 pounds in 10 months.

Again, Dr. McClelland at Harvard emphasizes that to reach your objectives, you must have accomplishment feedback. Every day I'd step on the scales and see a little less of me, so my confidence would grow for the next objective and the next one and the next one.

To go back to the cookware salesman, he was able to reach his objective because he had done something that's critically important: he had learned how to train fleas. I know you've heard the one about the two fleas at the bottom of the hill. One of them says to the other, "Well, do we walk or take a dog?"

In any event, you train fleas by putting them in a jar. Fleas jump. They'll jump up and hit the top. As they jump up and hit the top over and over, all of a sudden you'll notice something: even though they continue to jump, they're no longer hitting the top. Then you can take the top completely off. They'll keep on jumping, but they cannot jump out, because they've conditioned themselves to jump only just so high. Once that's happened, that's all there is. There ain't no more.

Humans are exactly the same. They start out in life to climb the mountain, to write the book, to break the record. They start out in life to do a lot of things. But along the way, they bump their heads. They stub their toes, and they become what I call a SNIOP: a person who is *susceptible to the negative influence of other people.* They start listening to the negative Nells and the negative Charlies of life who say you can't, you can't, you can't.

The four-minute mile is the perfect example. For years and years, athletes tried to run a mile in less than four minutes, and they couldn't, until 1954, when Roger Banister of Great Britain accomplished this feat. Then athletes the world over started running a mile in less than four minutes. Roger Banister was a flea trainer. Why couldn't other people do it before? Very simple. The coach had taken his stopwatch, put it on the athletes, and said, "You can't do it." The doctor had taken his stethoscope and said, "You can't do it. Your heart will come out of your body." They SNIOPed the athlete right out of the four-minute mile.

Then a flea trainer broke the barrier. Since then, hundreds of races have been run in less than four minutes. In Baton Rouge, Louisiana, in 1973, eight men ran under four minutes in the same race.

In case you've missed the point, a flea trainer is a person who is driven from within, who jumps out of the jar. A flea trainer understands that you can get everything in life you want if you will just help enough other people get what they want. A flea trainer doesn't try to see through people; a flea trainer sees people through. A flea trainer doesn't tell others where to get off; a flea trainer shows them how to get on. A flea trainer is convinced that inside of individuals there is an enormous amount of ability to go where they want to go, do what they want to do, be what they want to be, and have what they want to have.

Once you understand this principle, some amazing changes take place. The young cookware salesman I mentioned earlier was not suddenly possessed with a degree of genius; I know, because I'm talking about a younger brother. I know him very well, and I know that he did not suddenly gain an extra amount of intelligence. He simply possessed the goal and attitude that gave him enormous ability.

Do you want to reach your goals once you've set them? Then you've got to understand the story of Harry Houdini. Houdini was a master magician as well as a master locksmith. He boasted that he could get out of any jail cell in the world if you would let him walk into that cell with his street clothes on.

A small town in the British Isles had built a new jail. They were terribly proud of it. They issued Houdini a challenge: "Come, try to get out of our jail." Houdini responded to the challenge. There was a lot of publicity and a lot of money involved—and he liked them both. As he was driving into town, the drums were beating, the bugles were blaring, and there was an enormous crowd.

Houdini strode confidently into that jail. They closed the door behind him, and he took his coat off. Secreted in his belt was a ten-inch piece of steel—very tough, very flexible, very durable—and he went to work on the door.

In thirty minutes, that confident expression had disappeared. In an hour, he was drenched in perspiration. At the end of two hours, he collapsed against the door, which opened. It opened because it had never been locked anywhere except in his own mind. Which means that it was locked just as completely as if every locksmith in the world had put their best lock on it.

I tell that story because there are people wanting to open the door for you. They don't want to close it; they want to open it. Can you believe that your boss would love to give you a raise? Can you believe that your employer would like to pay you more money and promote you? But if I understand anything about free enterprise, your boss is not running a benevolent institution. He wants to pay you more money, but only if you become worth more to him.

This is going to shock you, but poorly paid people are relatively easy to find. It's the well-paid people who are difficult to find. In order to earn that kind of money, you've got to make that kind of a contribution.

I believe that inside of every human being is an enormous capacity. I believe man was designed for accomplishment. I believe he was engineered for success. I believe that he was endowed with the seeds of greatness. But if you're going to reach your goal, you've got to understand the story of the young sailor at sea.

It was in days of the sailing boat. The young man was at sea for the first time. A squall was coming up, and he'd been ordered to trim the sails. When he climbed up the mast, he made the mistake of looking down. He could see the roll of the ship and the turbulence of the sea, and he became nauseated. He lost his balance and started to fall. An older sailor beneath him said, "Look up, son. Look up." The young man immediately looked up and regained his balance.

The story simply says that when things don't look good—and that is going to happen in your life—make certain you're not looking in the wrong direction. When you're not looking at the sun, you see the shadows. If the outlook isn't good, try the uplook, because it's always good.

Want to reach your goal? Make up your mind you're going to reach it. A number of years ago, an international expedition was formed to climb the north wall of the Matterhorn. A reporter was interviewing the climbers. He went to one young man and asked, "Are you going to climb the north wall of the Matterhorn?"

"I'm going to give it a jolly good effort," he said.

The reporter went to another man and asked, "Are you going to climb the north wall?"

"I'm going to give it everything I've got," he said.

He went to another man and said, "Are you going to climb the north wall?"

"I'll be caught trying."

The reporter went to a young American and asked, "Are you going to climb the north wall of the Matterhorn—something that has never been done before?"

The young American said, "I will climb the north wall of the Matterhorn."

One man did. It was the man who said, "I will."

Want to reach your goal? You've got to see the reaching. I quit seeing myself as the 202-pound friendly fat boy. I started seeing myself as the friendly 165-pounder.

Major Nesmith's story says what I want to say. He was a golfer, and a lousy one. Shot in the 90s. As a matter of fact, he quit playing golf for over seven years; he didn't pick up a golf club. Then he went back to the golf course after a seven-year sabbatical, and the first time back he shot a 74. For those seven years, he was in the Hanoi Hilton, a prisoner of the North Vietnamese. For seven years, they kept his body in jail, but they did not confine his mind. For seven years, he played mental golf—eighteen full holes of it. He stroked the ball thousands and thousands of times. He never missed a shot. When he got back to the golf course, he did physically what he had been doing mentally for all those years. He saw the ball dropping in the cup. He saw the ball splitting the fairway. He saw success and success and success.

Do you want to reach your goals? Remember, finally, the story of the apostle Peter. I bet you remember old Peter. He was the enthusiastic one, the extrovert. Boy, with old Peter, nothing was just good; it was fantastic. Nothing was just bad; it was awful. No mediocre words for old Peter anywhere.

Then there's the story of Peter walking on water. The sea's not too smooth, but the Lord is walking on it. Old Peter said, "Lord, I would walk on water."

Christ simply said, "Come." Peter stepped out of the boat. I can see him in my mind's eye; I can see him stepping out there and walking. Then, the Scripture says, "when he saw the wind boisterous, he was afraid" (Matthew 14:30).

Did you ever wonder why Peter saw the wind boisterous? For one reason only: he took his eyes off the goal, Jesus Christ.

I don't care what your goal is. When you take your eye off the goal, you see the problem. If you want to reach your goal, you must keep your eye on the goal. Look at the solution and not the problem. Remember, you don't pay the price; you enjoy the price when you set and reach your goals. Which you can if you'll follow through.

As you have gone through this chapter, I hope you have carefully evaluated the purposes we set out. To refresh your memory and bring you back into perspective, let me remind you of those six purposes:

1. To sell you on the importance of goals in your personal and professional life.
2. To explain why most people never set goals.
3. To identify the kinds of goals you should have and their characteristics.
4. To elaborate on the characteristics of goals.
5. To spell out in specific detail how to set your goals.
6. To give detailed procedures for reaching your goals.

As I've said, success is not a destination; it's a journey. And you, my friend, are well on your way on your particular journey to the top.

8

Attitude

This chapter on attitude is extremely important. The reason is very simple: there is so much material, so much information, and so much need. There are also many solutions to the problems people encounter in their everyday lives.

The purposes of this chapter:

1. To demonstrate the importance of a right mental attitude.
2. To identify some of the many characteristics of attitude.
3. To protect your attitude against stinking thinking.
4. To give you a four-step formula on controlling your attitude, so that regardless of the circumstances, the foundation of your attitude is solid.
5. To point out that when you choose a habit, you also choose the end result of that habit.
6. To teach you how to avoid and/or eliminate destructive habits and acquire good ones.

A number of years ago, I was in Seattle, speaking to the Northwestern Lumbermens Association. You may wonder what need lumbermen might have for motivation. Let me tell you: whether you're a housewife, student, salesperson, or coach, everybody needs motivation. I suspect that you need a little bit of motivation to cut down trees.

I had been carefully instructed to tell a lot of stories. The boss said, "Zig, these men really like stories, so tell a lot of them."

When I was right in the middle of one of my stories, a big bruiser in about the tenth row stood right up and interrupted me. Now let me set the scene for you. The guy was about six feet, six inches tall and weighed about 250 pounds, as did most of the other guys. And his interruption was rather forceful.

As he stood up, he said, "Zig, I want to tell you a story."

I have a standard policy. When somebody six feet, six inches tall and weighing 250 pounds says, "I want to tell you a story," I generally grant them permission to do exactly that. So I said, "OK, friend. Sound off."

"I want to tell you about my buddy, Bill." He pointed to a little fellow next to him and said, "Stand up, Bill." Bill stood up, and he was about five feet and six inches tall, maximum. He couldn't have weighed over 130 pounds.

The first man said, "Old Bill came into camp here about a month ago. He walked up to me, stuck his hand out, and said, 'Shake hands with your new tree topper.' Now, Zig, I don't know if you know what a tree topper is or not. A tree topper is a fellow that climbs all the way to the top of the tree, saws the top of the tree off, and then hangs on for dear life. It ain't no job for a boy, that is for sure. So I looked at him, and I said, 'Bill, that is a man's job, and you're just a boy.'

"Well, old Bill just ripped his shirt off and said, 'I ain't a boy. I'm a man.' And, Zig, he was right. I have never seen so much muscle in one place in my life. This fellow is little, but he is all muscle. So he said, 'I'll tell you what I want you to do. Just give me a chance. Take me out to the woods, let me borrow an ax, and if I don't knock a tree down in less than half the time it takes your very best man to do it, I won't even ask for the job. But if I do, I want the job.'

"Shucks, Zig, I didn't have nothin' to lose. So I said, 'OK, you got yourself a deal.' I went out in the woods, picked out a spruce tree. It would have taken my best man at least thirty minutes to put it on the ground.

"Zig, I've never seen a man swing an ax in my life like little Bill. It was a solid sheet of steel back and forth. Why, in less than fifteen minutes, that tree was flat on the ground.

"I looked at him and said, 'Bill, where in the world did you learn how to cut down a tree like that?'

"Old Bill looked at me with those steel blue eyes and he said, 'In the Sahara.'

"'In the Sahara? Bill, the Sahara is a desert.'

"He looked at me again with those steel blue eyes and said, 'It is now.'"

You know what I believe? I believe that with the right mental attitude, we can build a business in the Sahara. I believe that with the right mental attitude, we can create prosperity, happiness, success, and love wherever we might be, whether it's in the Sahara Desert or the smallest town in America, whether it's in the biggest city or the most remote village. I believe that our thinking is going to play a tremendous part in that success.

I'm going to be completely honest with you: I'm going to be selling you on the advantages of the right mental attitude. You see, there are tens of thousands of schools in America. You can go to school and learn how to do just about everything, from trimming toenails to curling hair. You can learn how to take out tonsils or press a pair of trousers. You can learn how to run heavy equipment or drive a car. You can learn how to pull teeth or sell merchandise. You can learn how to get an A in school or be a better football player. You can learn virtually anything in some school in this country.

But there's not a human being or a school in existence that can teach you how to be any better than mediocre unless you've got the right mental attitude.

Many years ago, William James, the father of American psychology, said, "The most important discovery of our time is the discovery that we can alter our lives by altering our attitudes." First of all, he pointed out that attitude is extremely important, but he also said something that to me is even more significant: we are not stuck with the attitude that we now have. Regardless of whether it's good, bad, or indifferent, it is going to change. If it's bad or if it's indifferent, we can change it. If it's good, we can make it even better.

I want to start by talking about the optimist and the pessimist. I love what Dr. Robert Schuller has to say about the two. An optimist looks at a glass of water and figures it's half full. The pessimist looks at the glass of water and figures that it's half empty. But did you ever wonder why they look at it so differently? The pessimist has been drinking the water. He has been taking away; he's concerned that there's not going to be enough water for him. The optimist looks at that half glass of water and says it's half full because he's been filling it. He's been putting something in. He's been making a contribution, and he's confident that he's going to be able to fill it all the way to the top.

The optimist, according to Dr. Schuller, takes action. The pessimist takes a seat. The optimist rolls up his sleeves to get what he wants. The pessimist wrings his hands and loses what he had.

It's important to understand the difference that the right mental attitude can make. In sales, attitude makes the difference between making the sale and missing the sale. As any salesperson knows, the average commission you earn on the sales that you *almost* make is zero. There is a considerable difference between the commission you earn on the sale you make and the one you just barely make, yet there's so little difference between making the sale and missing the sale. It's a word, a phrase, a thought, an idea, an attitude. It's a little here and a little there, but that little bit makes an enormous difference to your bank deposits.

You might remember the story of the great racehorse Nashua. Nashua won over $1 million on the racetrack in less than one hour of racing. He had hundreds of hours of training and practice, but only one actual hour of racing.

Now you can take the $1 million that Nashua won, and you can buy 100 $10,000 racehorses. Now that is a fact. That's because a $1 million racehorse runs 100 times as fast as a $10,000 horse, right?

Do you agree with that? If not, ask yourself, how much faster a $1 million horse can run than a $10,000 horse. Is it twice as fast or 20 percent faster or 10 percent faster, or 2 percent faster? How much faster is a $1 million horse than a $10,000 one?

Years ago, at the Washington-Arlington Futurity Race, the winning horse received $100,000 more than the horse that came in second. Now this race was 1⅛ miles in length, which, as you well know, is 71,280 inches. The $100,000 winner finished that race exactly one inch ahead of the one that came in second. The race was 71,280 inches, but the one who won the $100,000 got there exactly one inch in front of the other. It's a little bit, but it does make an enormous amount of difference.

Similarly, in the 1974 Kentucky Derby, the winning jockey received $27,000 for riding the horse across the finish line ahead of all of the others. Slightly less than two seconds later, a horse crossed the line with a jockey aboard in fourth place. They wrote that jockey a check for $30. It was less than two seconds, but it made a difference of nearly $27,000.

Somebody asked me, "Is that right?" And I said, "No, it isn't right, but that's the way they do it. That's the way they've always done it, and that's the way they always will do it." There's no reward for almost booking a party, for almost making a sale, for almost getting there before the plane leaves.

There's no reward for *almost* doing anything. The reward comes from the accomplishment, and the difference between the accomplishment and the failure is minute. You can call a girl a kitten, and she'll love you. Call her a cat, you're in trouble. Say she's a vision, she'll smile all over. Call her a sight, and, friend, you've got a problem.

Or imagine a young fellow out courting one night. He looks in his girlfriend's eyes and says, "Honey, when I look into your eyes, the wheels of time just stand still." Beautiful. Poetry. But can you imagine the fellow looking into his girlfriend's eyes and saying, "Honey, you've got a face that'd stop a clock"?

I'll never forget the best definition of positive thinking I ever heard. Years ago, I flew back from a series of seminars to Atlanta, where we were living then. My family met me at the airport. As you might suspect, I do a large share of the talking in my family. As we were riding home, I was chatting away, telling my wife all of the good things that had happened. My six-year-old daughter was in the back seat with one of her little buddies. Out of the corner of my ear, I could hear the little buddy ask my daughter, "What does your daddy do?"

My daughter said, "Oh, he sells that positive thinking stuff."

"Positive thinking stuff? What in the world is that?"

"Oh," said my daughter, "You know: that's what makes you feel real good even if you feel real bad."

I've never heard a better definition of positive thinking.

What does positive thinking accomplish? Let's go back to a baseball game during the Depression years, between the Dallas team and the San Antonio team. They were minor league teams. In those days, minor league baseball was tremendously good, and it was the only recreation that many people had at that time. It was before the majors had expanded to so many teams, so the talent was great.

As a matter of fact, San Antonio had seven baseball players that had hit over .300 the year before. With seven men on the same team hitting over .300, everybody knew that San Antonio was going to win the pennant.

But a funny thing happened on the way to the pennant. The San Antonio team lost the first game, and the second, and the third, and the fourth, and the fifth. At the end of the twenty-first game, they had only won three.

The pitcher was blaming the outfielders. The outfielders were blaming the infielders. The infielders were blaming the catcher. The catcher was blaming the pitcher. It went round and round. Everybody was blaming everybody else, but the manager of the team knew what the problem was. He was a brilliant minor league manager. His name was O'Reilly.

O'Reilly knew that his team did not have any physical problems. They were suffering from stinkin' thinkin'. They needed a little checkup from the neck up, so he decided to try something unique.

San Antonio had played Dallas the day before, and Dallas had won, 1–0. The only hit the San Antonio team had gotten was a scratch single by the pitcher.

Now, the second day, they were going into the second game—same ballpark, same players, same conditions. But at this time in Dallas, there was a faith healer named Slater. It was said of Slater that he could do anything in this world, so O'Reilly conceived a plan.

About an hour before game time, O'Reilly came into the clubhouse and said, "Fellows, give me the best bats you've got, and put them in this wheelbarrow. When I come back, I'm going to have the solution to the day's game and to winning the pennant." Excited and motivated, he took those bats and left.

About five minutes before game time, O'Reilly came back into the clubhouse, pushing that wheelbarrow full of bats. Burning up with enthusiasm, he said, "I've taken these bats to Mr. Slater. He's put his blessings on them. He says all we've got to do is step up to the plate and take a cut at that old ball. He says there's no way we're going to miss. He says we're going to win the day today, and we're going to win the pennant. Don't worry about anything. Just go get 'em, Tigers."

What did those Tigers do? Well now, the day before remember they'd been beaten 1–0. They'd only gotten one hit. But today—with the same two teams, same ballpark, same circumstances—this team got 37 base hits, including 11 home runs. They scored 22 runs. I don't think I need to mention this, but they won the game. Of course, they won the pennant, by a tremendous margin.

For years after, Slater bats sold at an enormous premium all over the Texas League. If you could get ahold of a Slater bat, you were in good company. As a matter of fact, even though Slater allegedly saw only about twenty of the bats, hundreds and hundreds of Slater bats were sold throughout the

Texas League. But here's the rather intriguing thing: it was never proven that Slater had ever even seen the bats.

Just for the sake of discussion, let's assume that Slater had seen the bats. Even so, what in the world could a man do to a pile of wood? Absolutely nothing. But there was a tremendous amount he could do to the mind of the man who was swinging the wood, because the mind is going to complete the picture that you put into it.

If the batter steps up thinking, "I'm going to strike out," that's exactly what's going to happen. If the batter steps up saying, "I'm going to get a hit," the odds go up dramatically.

The mind completes the picture that we put into it. We go out to make a sale, and we come back and say, "I sold it. I knew I would." Others come back and say, "I knew that was a lousy prospect. I missed it. I knew I would."

One attitude that I want to talk about is enthusiasm. Attitude is extremely important. Many people go through life in reverse, meaning that when things are going well, they've got a fantastic attitude; their enthusiasm is sky-high. When things are bad, their attitude is miserable; their enthusiasm is down.

I'm going to say unequivocally that that is the exact reverse of what it ought to be. We need to build a solid attitude foundation. When things are going extremely well, our attitude is good. When things are going extremely badly, our attitude is still good, because soon things are going to be good. Under that formula, things are not controlling your attitude; your attitude is controlling your performance.

Let me give you an example of what I'm talking about. In Pine Bluff, Arkansas, there's a grocery chain called The Mad Butcher. It got its name because the butcher, Allan Bellamy, was buying neck bones for 15 cents a pound and selling them for a dime. The man who was selling them to him said, "That's mad. You can't do that." Allan laughed and said, "That fits perfectly, because I am the mad butcher," and the name was born.

Allan started the store right after the Korean War. When he came back, his mother had a little mom-and-pop grocery store. As Allan described it, you opened the front door, and it banged against the meat market, which was at the back door. In other words, it wasn't a big store.

But business was good. As a matter of fact, it was so good that they soon had to expand their operation. They went to the bank, and despite limited resources, they were able to borrow $95,000 to build a supermarket shell. They were a tremendous and instant success. They were so successful that every supermarket chain in America apparently heard about what was going on down in Pine Bluff, and within the next six months ten new supermarket chains were opened there.

Allan told me, "Zig, every time a new store would open, I could feel my business being sucked out the front door. Man, you could shoot a shotgun down the center of our aisle and never be in danger of hitting anybody. Business was bad. We were doing less business in our big store than we'd been doing in the little one."

"Then," Allan said, "someone came by, selling the Dale Carnegie course. I told him, 'Friend, if it didn't cost but 50 cents for me to go around the world, I couldn't get out of sight. I'm broke. I can't buy anything else. I can't take any more training.'"

But, Allan said, the man used a little analogy: "'Did you hear the one about the woodcutter whose production kept going down because he didn't take time to sharpen his ax?' So he convinced me. We went to the bank. We borrowed the money, and five of us took the course.

"The fifth session is on enthusiasm. At the end of that session, we determined that we were going to be ten times as enthusiastic as we had ever been about anything. We were really going to be on fire.

"The next morning, in walks this unsuspecting little housewife to maybe buy a loaf of bread and pick up a can of beans and a few other things. Innocently she grabs the basket, but at that moment, our cashier converged on her, our butcher converged on her, our store manager converged on her, our bag boys converged on her. Everybody rushed out to welcome her into the store.

"You know, it's a funny thing, Zig. The people in town who had thought I was the mad butcher now knew that I was. But without changing anything else in our entire operation, within two weeks our business had moved from $15,000 a week to in excess of $30,000 a week. It has never fallen below that."

Enthusiasm works: a dozen or so years later, The Mad Butcher had twenty-six supermarkets in full swing, doing in excess of $45 million worth of business.

You would have to work night and day from now on to forever to convince me that enthusiasm was not a key factor in success. I believe that your business is never either good or bad *out there*. Your success, your happiness, is not *out there*. All of these things are either good or bad, successful or unsuccessful, right between your own two ears. If you're suffering from stinkin' thinkin', you're going to have stinkin' everything else too. I can guarantee it.

At one point I was speaking for a group of realtors in Flint, Michigan. Before I started to speak, there was a luncheon. I was seated next to a little guy on my left, and we'd chatted along pleasantly for a few minutes. Then I made the cardinal mistake that day: I said, "How's your business?"

For the next ten minutes, he elaborated on just how bad business was: "Mr. Ziglar, you know, General Motors is on strike. In Flint, Michigan, which is a General Motors town, when General Motors is on strike, nobody buys anything from anybody. They don't buy any shoes or clothes. They don't even buy any food, so they surely don't buy any real estate. It's so bad that if something is not done almost immediately, I'm going to go bankrupt. I haven't written a contract in so long I doubt that I'd even remember how to fill out the paperwork." He was the kind of guy that could brighten up a whole room by leaving it. Or, like this old boy down home would say, he could frequently be overheard saying nothing.

Finally, somebody saved the day by coming up and asking him a question, so I turned to the little gal on my right. Cute little gal, about sixty years old, four feet, nine or ten inches tall—couldn't have weighed over eighty pounds soaking wet.

I asked, "How's everything?" I think you'll agree that gave her a lot of leeway.

Guess what she said? "You know, Mr. Ziglar, General Motors is on strike." I thought, "I have done it again," but she finished with the most beautiful smile I think I have ever seen in my life.

This woman grinned as if she'd just walked through a swinging door on somebody else's push, and she said, "Everything is fantastic. For the first time in months, people have plenty of time to go shopping for the home of their dreams. Why, they'll spend all day sometimes looking at just one or two houses. They go up in the attic, check the insulation, measure every square inch of floor space, check the closets, check the foundation. They check everything. They've got nothing else to do.

"These people are intelligent. They know the strike's going to end. They have faith in America's economy, and they know that right now, they can buy a house cheaper than they're ever going to be able to buy one again. I'm selling them by the ton."

Then the lady got confidential. She said, "Mr. Ziglar, do you know anybody down in Washington?"

"Why, yes, ma'am. I sure do," I said. "As a matter of fact, I've got a nephew in school down there right now."

"Oh, no. I mean, do you know anybody down there that's got some political muscle?"

"No, I don't, but why do you ask?"

"I was just thinking, if you knew somebody down there that could keep this strike going just for six more weeks, that's all I need, and I could quit for the year."

I give you my word that this story is true in every detail. One realtor was going broke because the strike was on. Another was getting rich because the strike was on. You see, it's not the situation out there; it's the situation right between your own two ears that makes such an enormous difference.

There's another attitude that I want to touch on. Now I'm all for the go-getter. As a matter of fact, one of my favorite go-getters is this old boy down home. It was long ago and down home, in Yazoo City, Mississippi. It has a river running right through it: the Yazoo River. This old boy used to run a ferry across that river, and he'd charge passengers 10 cents for a ride across that river. One day, someone asked him, said, "How many trips a day do you make?"

"I make as many as I possibly can, because the more I go, the more I get. If I don't go, I don't get."

It's just about that simple. Yes, I'm enthusiastic about the go-getter, but I'm also enthusiastic about the go-giver. I'd like to share something with you that I think is very significant. In my judgment, the outstanding story of the twentieth century is the story of Israel. This nation was founded in 1948 amid political discord, disruptions, and incredible barriers. Jewish people from all over the world came to Israel. In many cases, they had waited 2,000 years to get out of the ghetto.

Now I've just used the word *ghetto* and not *slum*. There's a vast difference. The ghettos, where the Jews were, had barricades. They could not get out physically. The slum is a deplorable condition to live in. Although we unfortunately find many of these in America, there are no restraining walls. People can get out of the slums, and that's a very significant difference.

For 2,000 years, the Jews had waited to come to their homeland. They came from all over the world to found the nation of Israel. They came to gain religious freedom. They came because this was the homeland that had been promised to them. They came to get, but they did not come looking for a free lunch. They came to give something in the process, and the results have been the wonder of this century. They took the desert, added water by irrigating, and created high-producing vineyards. They added ingenuity to hard work and attracted business and tourists from all over the world. They added commitment, pride, and the go-give spirit to a population of which a large portion are of the Arab world. With all of this, they have been able to withstand the power of all the combined Arab nations.

I think this is the most exciting story of this century. The Jews came to give and to get, and in the process, they did both. Incidentally, Israel has the lowest crime rate of any of the Western nations. Vandalism is unknown in that nation, because builders are not destroyers, and destroyers are seldom builders.

In Israel, everybody serves the state for a period of time. When a young boy or girl is called up but rejected by the military, instead of being delighted (as, unfortunately, many of our citizens are over here), mother and dad immediately show up at the draft board and say, "What's the matter with my son? What's the matter with my daughter? Why can't they serve? They're just as good as anybody else. There's something you can find for them to do. They want to do their part." That's what makes the nation an absolute marvel.

The go-give spirit is important. Did you know that North and South America were founded for two entirely different reasons? South America was entered, explored, and populated for the sole purpose of taking the gold and going back. North America was populated by people who came seeking religious freedom. They came and founded this continent on the principles of Almighty God. All you've got to do is look at the economic record, and you will see the difference between those two.

One reason I love my Bible so much is that it's full of positive thinking. You're no doubt familiar with the story of David and Goliath, but you're now going to get the Ziglarized version.

There's old Goliath, nine feet tall, weighing 400 pounds. He's walking around on the hillsides, shouting and cussing and screaming: "You dogs, come on out and fight."

Here comes little David, seventeen years old. He sees that giant and says to his brothers, "Don't you hear that guy?"

"Yeah, we hear him."

"What you going to do about it?"

"Are you kidding? Why, people get hurt fighting fellas like that."

David said, "Where's the king?"

"The king don't feel so good."

"Well, I'll take him on."

They said, "You are crazy." They looked at Goliath and figured he was too big to hit. David looked at him and figured he was too big to miss.

You know how this story turned out. In any case, I was reading it to my son, who was eight at the time. I said, "David was really a brave boy, wasn't he, son?"

"Yeah, Dad, David was brave, but it was Goliath that was the brave one."

"How do you figure that?"

"Well, Daddy," he said, "you've got to understand. Goliath was out there all by himself. David had God with him." You know, the boy was right.

Here's another story. I was once in New York teaching an adult education class, and we had a gentleman in that class. His name was Ed Green. I never will forget him: a very distinguished looking man, apparently in his sixties. He sold advertising. I don't know Ed's exact income, but they told me that it was well over $75,000 a year. This was back in the 1950s. That would be a great deal more money today.

Yet there he was, in a class learning about selling. One evening, I just couldn't resist the question. "Ed, I'm a little puzzled," I said. "There are three instructors in this class, and our combined income is not as great as yours. Yet here you are, the most enthusiastic guy of them all. Why are you in this class?"

"Well, Zig," he said, "it's something that my dad told me when I was a boy. Dad was a gardener. One of the greatest I've ever seen. He took enormous pride in that garden. One day, trying to get me interested in helping him, he took me out in the garden and walked me through it. He pointed out all the beautiful, green, growing things.

"When we finished, he turned to me and said, 'Ed, what did you learn?'

"Zig, all I'd learned was that Dad had obviously done an awful lot of hard work. So I said, 'Dad, I just learned that you do have a pretty garden.'

"Dad said, 'Son, what I wanted you to notice was this: as long as everything in that garden was green, it was still growing. But the moment it got ripe, it started to rot.'"

Quite a lesson. Think about that for a moment. In the game of life, when we stop growing and developing, we grow old. I know people well over ninety years old who are keen, sharp, alert, enthusiastic, and motivated. I know people in their forties who are old men and women because they've refused to let their minds expand.

Many times, that happens when they get out of college. I've seen it in girls who were beautiful in high school. I've seen those same girls thirty years later, and I wondered what in the world had happened to them. Then I would see another girl who was a plain Jane in high school and a beautiful woman twenty-five or thirty years later. The first woman accepted natural beauty as hers forever and waited for the world to come and serve her. The plain one often went out and did the extra. Over the years, she grew and developed.

The rest of the Ed Green story is even more exciting. Ed smiled at me and said, "You know, Zig, many of the things I've learned here I haven't really learned; I've just relearned. But because of a technique that I picked up in this class, I recently closed a sale that I had been working on for over three years. That one sale will more than pay for all of the education about selling and motivation I have had for all of the years."

By now it's obvious that I believe attitude is tremendously important. But there's an aspect of attitude that a lot of people never take into consideration: how do we react to particular situations?

We cannot tailor-make a situation that's going to prevail all through our lifetime, but we can tailor-make an attitude in advance that will fit any situation that comes up. Now this I fervently believe. We have to learn how to react to a lot of things and react to them properly. I believe the story of Mr. B says exactly what I want to say.

Once Mr. B, a company owner, called a meeting of all of his people and said, "I noticed that some of you come in to work late. Some of you are spending too much time on a coffee break or lunch break. Maybe that's not your fault. Maybe that's my fault. Maybe I've not set for you the kind of an example that I should have been setting, so in the future, I'm going to be the kind of leader you can follow. I'm going to get here early and stay late. I'm going to take short coffee breaks and short lunch breaks. I'm going to provide the kind of leadership that will enable us to build a marvelous company."

It was quite a little speech, and his intentions were good. But about four days later, he was out at the local country club for lunch, and he became engrossed in the business conversation. He forgot about the time and all of a sudden looked at his watch. He said, "Oh, my goodness. I'm due back at the office in ten minutes."

Mr. B made a mad dash to his automobile, hopped in, and burned rubber. He was going ninety miles an hour down the freeway when the long arm of the law entered the picture and gave him a ticket.

Mr. B was furious. He said, "This is ridiculous. Here I am, a peaceful taxpayer, a law-abiding citizen, minding my own business, and what does this guy do? He comes along and gives me a ticket. He ought to be out looking for the robbers, the murderers, the arsonists, the people who are breaking the law. He ought to leave us peaceful taxpayers alone." Oh, he was really upset.

By the time Mr. B got back to the office, about an hour and a half late, he did what management has done since the beginning of time: every time they get their hand caught in the cookie jar, they say, "Look yonder."

In a very loud voice, Mr. B called for the sales manager. He said, "Come on in here. I want to talk to you about the Armstrong account right now. You've been fooling with that thing for six weeks, and I just want you to tell me in one simple word that yes, you made the deal, or no, you did not make the deal."

The sales manager ducked his head, walked in the office, and very meekly and quietly closed the door behind him. He said, "Mr. B, I can tell you this: I thought I had that sale. I thought it was mine. I thought it was all signed, sealed, and delivered. But you know what? At the last minute, something happened, and it came unglued. I don't know what happened, Mr. B, but I lost the sale."

If you think Mr. B was unhappy before, you should have seen him now. He was furious. He said, "This is ridiculous. For eighteen years, you've been my sales manager. For eighteen years, I've depended on you to bring in new business. Now we have a chance to get the biggest account of all, and what do you do? You blow it. Well, let me tell you, friend, just because you've been here for eighteen years does not mean that you've got a life-time contract. I'm going to tell you this one time and one time only: you replace that business, or I'm going to replace you." Oh, he was really upset.

But if you think Mr. B was upset, you should have seen that sales manager. He left far from quietly. He walked through the door and slammed it behind him, muttering, "This is ridiculous. For eighteen years I've been running this company. I'm the only one who knows what's going on around here. If it hadn't been for me, they would have gone down the tube fifteen years ago. Now, just because I lost one miserable deal, he uses a cheap, cotton-picking trick, and he threatens to fire me. This is not fair." Oh, he was really upset.

The sales manager called his secretary in a very loud voice, and said, "Remember those five letters I gave you this morning? Have you gotten them out? Have you been fiddling around with something else that's not important at all?"

The secretary said, "What? No, don't you remember? You told me that the Hilliard account took precedence over everything else, and that's what I've been working on. So, no, I have not had a chance to get those letters out."

"Look, don't give me any lousy excuses. I told you I wanted those let-ters out, and I want them out today. I'm just going to tell you this one time. If you can't get them out today, I'm going to get somebody that can. Just because you've been here eight years does not mean that you've got a life-time contract." Oh, he was really upset.

But if you think the sales manager was upset, you should have seen that secretary. She went out of his office and slammed the door behind her back, muttering, "This is ridiculous. For eight years I've been at this company. As a matter of fact, I'm the only one who knows what's going on around here. Why, if it hadn't been for me, this company would've gone down the tubes seven years ago. Now, just because I can't do two things at once, he uses a cheap, lousy trick: he threatens to fire me. After all the hundreds of hours of overtime work I've done without ever getting a dime in overtime pay. Who does he think he's kidding anyhow?" Oh, she was really upset.

The secretary walked up to the switchboard operator and said, "Look, I've got five letters. Just get them out. Now I know ordinarily that's not your job, but you don't do anything but sit out here and answer the telephone. I want you to get these letters out. And I'm going to tell you this just one time: if you can't get them out, I'm going to get somebody who can." Oh, she was really upset.

But if you think the secretary was upset, you should have seen that switchboard operator. She said, "This is ridiculous. Why, I'm the only one who knows what's going on around here. They don't do anything in the back but gossip, drink coffee, talk on the telephone, and maybe get a little bit of work out. The minute they get behind, they come out here, throw something down on my desk, and say, 'Now you're going to get this out, or we're going to fire you.' Why, if it hadn't been for me, they'd have gone down the tube five years ago. This is ridiculous."

The switchboard operator was really upset, but she got the letters out. When she got home, she was still furious. She walked in the front door and slammed it behind her, muttering under her breath all the time. The first thing she saw was her twelve-year-old son lying on the floor watching television. The second thing she saw was a big rip right across the seat of his britches. She said, "Son, how many times have I told you, when you come home from school, put your play clothes on? Mother has a hard enough time as it is supporting you and sending you through school. Now just for that, you're going to go upstairs right now. There's going to be no supper for you tonight. No television for the next three weeks."

Oh, the operator was really upset. But if you think she was upset, you should have seen that twelve-year-old boy. He hopped up, muttering under his breath, "This is ridiculous. I was doing stuff for my mother. She didn't give me a chance to explain. I had an accident; it could happen to anybody. This is not fair, and she didn't even give me a chance to explain."

About that time, his tomcat walked in front of him, which was a mistake. The boy gave the tomcat a big old boot and said, "You get out of here. You've probably been up to no good yourself."

If you think about it for a moment, that tomcat was the only creature involved that could not have altered that series of events. If you think about it just that much longer, wouldn't it have been better if Mr. B had just gone directly from the country club to the operator's house and kicked that cat himself?

Now I've got a couple of questions to ask you. Whose cat have you been kicking lately? Have you been letting somebody else kick your cat? What I'm really saying is, how do you react to a negative situation? How do you react to a putdown? How do you react to rudeness? How do you react to unkindness? How do you react to disappointment?

All of us can react positively and pleasantly when somebody's nice to us, smiles at us, or gives us an order (providing it's a sales order). But how do we react to the negative situations of life?

Why should you let anybody else determine the way you act? The bum on the Bowery and the most successful man in existence have a great deal in common. There isn't a human being, including those at the top of their field, who has not suffered many frustrations, disappointments, setbacks, and defeats. But the successful man or woman does not react negatively to the negative. The bum on the Bowery suffers disappointment; he tries to drown the problem and in the process drowns his future.

We can condition ourselves to react positively to a negative situation. But how do most people react? Have you ever gone into a restaurant to get a cup of coffee and sat there and sat there? Finally, you timidly hold your hand up and say, "Could I have a cup of coffee?" How do you react when the waitress says, "Can't you see I'm busy? I'll get to you in just a minute." You say, "You don't have to bite my head off about it, do you?"

How do you react in this situation? You've had a magnificent day: sales have been extraordinarily good. You come home that evening floating in that front door, and ask, "Hi, honey, how are you doing?" Your spouse says, "Where in the world have you been? You're supposed to have been here twenty minutes ago. If you'd been putting up with everything I've been putting up with all day, you would know how I've been doing."

Can you understand that this has nothing in the world to do with you? Somebody's been kicking your spouse's cat all day long.

You go out to sell something, and the prospect slams the door in your face. How do you react? Can you understand that in ninety-nine cases out of 100 it's got nothing to do with you? Somebody else has kicked that person's cat before you ever got there. Or you check out of a motel, and the clerk takes your head off. Can you understand that has absolutely nothing in the world to do with you?

The way you react is tremendously important in whatever you do, because that reaction is going to determine exactly what you're going to do with your life. What is your upset point? How high you go is largely determined by your upset point. If a minor thing gets you upset, you've got a problem.

What is your upset point? What can you do about it?

Let me tell you one little thing you can do: next time somebody starts to chew you out, let them finish the chewing. The Bible says, "He that answereth a matter before he heareth it, it is folly and shame unto him" (Proverbs 18:13). Don't interrupt them. Let them finish the chewing. It'll make them feel better and gets the steam out of the way. Maybe somewhere along the way there is a degree of validity in what they're saying, so maybe you ought to listen for that reason. But let me suggest that you do this, especially if you know you're innocent (and of course you know you're innocent): pat your foot and say to yourself, "Cat, cat, cat." It's awfully hard to get upset while you're saying, "Cat, cat, cat." You just can't do it.

Finally, when they finish—I'm going to suggest that you try this first of all with your mate—why don't you look at them and say, "Honey, let me ask you a question. Has anybody been kicking your cat today?"

If you survive that one, then try it on the general public. It's awfully hard to get irritated at somebody who responds like that. In the general public, though, when you ask somebody if anyone has been kicking their cat, don't be too surprised if they say, "What do you mean, kicking my cat? I haven't even got one."

If they miss the point, understand this: in the game of life, we frequently lose. People often say no when we want them to say yes. Sometimes we strive mightily and still don't reach our objectives. How do you react to the disappointment?

The way you respond to defeat is terribly important. Did you know that it's a positive sign if a failure temporarily depresses you? If it did not take some of the wind out of your sails, if it did not get you down a little bit, that would indicate that you did not care whether you won or lost. If you don't care whether you win or lose, I'm going to welcome you to the club of losers, because these are the people who lose.

Furthermore, if you learn from defeat, you haven't really lost. In addition, remember that you do not drown by falling in water. You only drown if you stay there. You do not fail by getting beaten occasionally. You only fail if it brings you down and keeps you down.

There are no hopeless situations; there are only some people who will lose hope in the face of some situations. The darkest night since the beginning of time did not turn out all the stars. I don't care what the situation is; there is some good in it.

Before we go any further, let me ask you a question: do you know anybody who is not as intelligent, not as attractive, not as well educated, not as hardworking as you, but has more money and friends and has more fun? If the answer is yes—and I'll bet you that it is—then would you agree with me that maybe, just maybe, it could be because of these people's attitude?

Many times, the brightest student doesn't make the best grades, because they don't have the right learning attitude. Sometimes the student only seeks a grade. If that's all they want, they'll get it. But if they seek the education, they'll get the grades as well as the education.

An attitude can be both caught and taught. We know that we can catch the flu; all we've got to do is be exposed to it. But you can also catch a good case of the poverties. All you've got to do is be with and around enough people with the poverties, and you'll end up with a rip-roaring case of it yourself. Get around enough people who've got negative thinking, and that's exactly what you are going to end up with yourself. Negative thinking can be caught, and it can be taught. Morals can be caught and also taught.

Attitude is that important. Andrew Carnegie once brought one of the greatest steel men in the world over from the Krupp Iron Works in Germany—reputedly the foremost authority in the world on the manufacture of steel. Carnegie gave him a five-year contract, moved him from Germany, bought him a home over here, set him up, and six months later paid off the contract and moved him back to Germany. The man was technically brilliant, but his attitude was permeating the entire organization, and Carnegie simply did not want it in his company. He wanted to get rid of that stinkin' thinkin'.

How, then, do we get and keep the right mental attitude? Regardless of the national or local situation, regardless of our friends, regardless of the weather, regardless of our own business, regardless of anything else, how do we keep and maintain that right mental attitude? That's a question that everybody wants answered.

If at this moment a young man burst into your house and said, "I want to sell you some insurance," chances are that you would resent the interruption.

But suppose the young man were to say, "Wait a minute. I'm not selling life insurance, health insurance, or liability insurance. I'm selling attitude insurance. It's the most fantastic insurance policy in existence. I can guarantee you that if you buy the policy, your attitude will be good, and it will be on the way to getting better."

Would you like to find out what kind of an insurance policy that young man was selling? Would you be interested in buying it? Would you be willing to pay, say, $5 a week, if you knew that your attitude was going to be good and getting better every single day?

You might think, "I'd give $100 a week for it." You might even think, "Boy, if I could get a policy like that, there's nothing I wouldn't give for it, because that's the answer right there."

I've got the best news for you you've had in a long time. I'm going to describe in minute detail exactly what that insurance policy is, because it's in a formula form. It won't cost you any additional money, take any of your time, or require any more effort than is required to bring in a sack of groceries from the car. It's quite a formula. I'll guarantee it.

I'm going to tell you in advance that if you'll follow the formula, two things will happen: you'll make more money, and you'll have more fun than you've ever had in your life. Before I go any further, have you already decided, "I don't know what that formula is, but if I can make more money and have more fun, and if it's not going to cost me any money or take any of my time, I'm going to follow that formula"?

Let me make an apparent digression. If I were to come into your home with a pail of garbage and dump it on your living room floor, chances are I'd have trouble in a hurry. You'd either whip me, call the law and have me arrested, or get your gun and say, "Now, Ziglar, I'll just bet you can clean that mess up." The chances are pretty strong that you're exactly right. Not only would I clean it up, but I would do it quickly, and I'd do an excellent job.

For weeks and months afterward, you'd be telling everyone about the nut that came in your house and threw garbage on the floor. You'd say, "I ought to have shot the dude. As a matter of fact, I wish I had." The very idea of somebody coming along and throwing garbage on your living room floor! Yet you can take modern cleaners and completely remove all traces of the garbage.

What about the people that come along and inadvertently, and on occasion deliberately, dump negative garbage in your mind? How do you react to that? Do you just sit there, smile, and say, "Yeah, that's right. Things are tough all over. It's awful. The country's going to the dogs. Yeah, dump the garbage in. It doesn't bother me."

If you're laboring under the illusion that what is dumped into your mind is not going to be detrimental or supportive, depending on whether it's positive or negative, you are 100 percent wrong. Your mind works exactly like a garden: whatever you plant is going to come up. You don't plant beans to raise potatoes. You plant beans to raise beans. It's the law of the universe. The Bible says, "As you sow, so also shall you reap." You plant a bean, however, not to raise a bean, but to raise a bunch of beans. You plant a potato to raise a bunch of potatoes. Between the time you plant and the time of harvest, the fertilizer, the nourishment in the soil, the sunshine, and the rain multiply the planting. Otherwise, there'd be no reason to plant.

The mind does exactly the same thing. Whatever you plant in your mind will come up in multiples. If you plant a negative thought, one negative does not come up; a bunch of negatives come up. Thank goodness it works on the other side too. If you plant a positive, a lot of positives will also come up. What kind of seeds are we going to be planting in our minds? The planting of the seed will determine the harvest later on.

I might also emphasize that your mind is exactly like a bank. You go down to the bank, and there are two tellers down there: a positive teller and a negative teller. You can make a deposit in a bank. Generally, you are the only person who is going to make a deposit in your bank account. And unless there's a forger around, you are the only one who's going to be making the withdrawal.

The bank of the mind does not work that way. Anybody and anything at any time can make a series of deposits. The radio makes deposits. The television makes deposits. The neighbors make deposits. Your friends, your relatives, strangers, acquaintances, everybody, comes along and makes deposits in the bank of your mind.

Even though everybody makes those deposits in your mind bank, you and only you can make the withdrawals. So what kind of withdrawals are you going to make?

You will have a strong tendency to withdraw directly from the latest deposit that was made in your mind, whether it was positive or negative, humorous or sad, exhilarating or demoralizing.

This tells us that we should be very careful to keep the good deposits going into our mind on a fresh and daily basis. If the deposit has been pornographic, critical, caustic, or negative, you will tend to withdraw from that.

Here is the only thing that overrides this pattern: if a lifetime of depositing has been taking place, those deposits will tend to override the latest one. Which deposit is the biggest? Which is the strongest? Was the deposit one of honesty or dishonesty? Was it moral or immoral? Was it wasteful or thrifty? Bold or cautious? Lazy or industrious? Positive or negative?

You are the sum total of what goes into your mind over a period of years. If you had been born in China, spoken the Chinese language, and been fed Chinese ideology over a long period of time, you would become Chinese in every respect except in the actual blood that flows through your body. You are in fact the sum total of everything that goes into your mind.

In this mind bank of ours, we make deposits over a period of time which constitute what is familiarly known as our memory. When you've got a problem, you go either to the positive or to the negative teller. You go to the positive teller, for example, and say, "Look, I've got a problem. Can you give me some information on how I can handle this particular problem?"

The positive teller says, "Certainly. Don't you remember? You were confronted with identically the same situation just six months ago, and you handled it just as smoothly as glass. You did a magnificent job. Why don't you try the same thing?"

You say, "Hey, thank you, Mr. Positive Teller. That's what I think I'm going to use, but I need a little more information to go along with that."

The positive teller comes back and says, "Remember when you were in the fifth grade? Such and such a thing happened, and you handled it this way. Just three weeks ago, you were confronted with a situation, and here's the way you handled it. Six months ago, you did it this way. A year ago, you did it this way. Every time, you are the person who always succeeds, and this is the way you've done it."

Then you say, "Thank you, Mr. Positive Teller. That's all I need, and I'll go solve the problem now." That's what memory really is.

But suppose you go to the negative teller and say, "Hey, I've got a problem. If you remember, I really fumbled the ball just three weeks ago on this. As a matter of fact, I looked like an idiot. Can you reinforce that for me and convince me again that I'm not very bright and I'm probably going to end up making the same mistake?"

The negative teller says, "Certainly. That's easy. Remember, at a party just six months ago you were confronted with a situation, and you really made an idiot of yourself that night. Not only that, but just three days earlier you'd done exactly the same thing. As a matter of fact, ever since you were a child, you've had this problem over and over. There is no way that you're ever going to be able to come up with a proper solution."

Then you say, "Thank you, Mr. Negative Teller. That's what I was afraid of all the time."

In short, over a period of time, the words, thoughts, and actions that go into our mind do affect our thinking. Thinking in turn affects and controls our actions.

For example, over the years, they've spent millions of dollars on a cure for the common cold, and so far they've come up with two conclusions: they don't know what causes it, and they don't know how to cure it. But this they have discovered beyond any reasonable doubt: when we are emotionally down or depressed, we are far more likely to catch the common cold than at any other time. Stinkin' thinkin' does cause all kinds of problems, including the common cold.

Let me give you an intriguing example of how thinking affects our lives. In 1969, a man named Charlie Ritter, who lived in Sac City, Iowa, had cancer. He had a kidney removed, and the surgeons thought they had gotten all of it, but three months later they discovered a lump in each of his lungs. His physical condition was such that the doctor said that he was not physically strong enough to withstand an operation.

At that time, Mayo Clinic was experimenting with a new drug. They said to Charlie Ritter, "If you would like, we'll run the experiment on you. But we want you to know that only 10 percent of the people who have taken this drug have had any results at all. In every case, those people that it worked on have always been over sixty years old."

Charlie Ritter qualified there: he was over sixty years old. He said, "I've got nothing to lose and everything to gain. Give me the drug." They administered the drug on the condition that if and when he did die, regardless of whether it was six months or ten years later, he would be willing to have them perform an autopsy on his body.

Charlie Ritter said, "I'll do it. There's no problem there." The agreement was made. A few months later, he was hale and hearty. He died six years later, of a heart attack. The surgeons who performed the autopsy could find no trace of cancer anywhere in his body.

The doctors told Charlie's family the rest of the story: The drug worked only on people over sixty, but with two qualifications. Number one, they fervently believed that the drug was going to work on them. Number two, they had a tremendous desire to live.

There's no way I can overstate the importance of what goes into our minds. In 1972, after a two-year study, the Surgeon General of the United States concluded that there was a definite relationship between televised violence and antisocial behavior. Dr. Albert Bandura and Dr. Leonard Berkowitz at the University of Wisconsin and Stanford University determined that children are more susceptible and therefore more likely to respond to this influence. Dr. Berkowitz then observed that people who watch sex movies are certain to be sexually active afterward.

As I've already observed, you withdraw from the latest deposit. What goes in the mind comes out of the mind. What we put in that mind has a tremendous bearing on what we do in our lives.

You may know a couple who was married for five years, ten years, or even more, but didn't have any children. As they started to get old, somebody said to them, "You'd better adopt a baby, because one of these days you're going to be too old, and they won't even let you adopt one."

The couple goes down and adopts a baby. They come home holding that baby in their hands. Then a friend or relative comes up to them and says, "Wouldn't it be funny if the same thing happened to you that happened to my sister? She'd been married for twenty-three years. The doctor said they couldn't have a baby. They adopted one, and now, less than six months later, they find out they're going to have one all on their own."

Somebody else says, "I've got a cousin in Albuquerque. She'd been married for twenty-one years. The doctor said they couldn't have a baby. They adopted, and it wasn't two years before they had one all on their own."

Other friends tell the couple similar stories. The deposits going into the mind begin to change. Instead of saying, "We can't, we can't, we can't," they say, "Wouldn't it be funny if... After all, those other people did. Maybe the same thing will happen to us."

Please don't misunderstand. Some people physiologically cannot have children. But for everyone who physiologically cannot give birth, there are probably a dozen or more who do not give birth to a child for psychological reasons.

What goes in the mind does have an effect. What we see, what we hear, and what we read become tremendously important for our conduct. The statement that if you do not live the life you believe, you will believe the life you live is more than just a cliché.

Nothing is absolute in this world of ours but God's law. But generally, if you associate with winners and highly moral people, you will be influenced and will become that way.

I was intrigued to read a story in a Dear Abby column that I could entitle "The Development of a Criminal." When Johnny was six, he was with his father, who was caught speeding. He saw his father hand the officer a $5 bill with his driver's license. There was no ticket. When Johnny was ten, he broke his glasses on the way to school. He heard his mother tell the man from the insurance company that they had been stolen, and they collected $27. When Johnny was fifteen, he made right guard on the high school football team. His coach taught him to block while grabbing the opposing end by the shirt so the official couldn't see it. When he was sixteen, he took a summer job at a big market. His job was to put the overripe tomatoes at the bottom of the boxes and the good ones on top.

When Johnny went to college, he was approached by an upper classman who offered him the answers to an English examination for $3. "It's OK, kid," he was told. "Everybody does it."

Johnny was caught and sent home in disgrace. "How could you do this to your mother and me?" his father asked. "You never learned anything like this at home."

Similarly, the correlation between parents' use of tobacco and alcohol and the kids' use of drugs has been firmly established.

When you choose what goes in your mind, you choose what you will become. If in your past you've been feeding the wrong things into your mind, if you've acquired some bad habits, if you've dealt with the wrong crowd, if you have not been as successful as you wish, then let me simply say that at this moment, we could break out in song. We could sing "Happy Birthday" to you, because today is the first day of the rest of your life.

9

Building Enthusiasm

Now I'm going to tell you exactly how to build and keep up enthusiasm. Everybody on the face of this earth is enthusiastic. There's never been a human being who was not enthusiastic. Now some of them only are enthusiastic for a minute a year, some for two minutes a year, and some thirty minutes a year, but everybody is enthusiastic. The length of time you're enthusiastic will be the determining factor.

Is enthusiasm important? I believe it's the difference between a great salesperson and just a good one. I believe it's the difference between a great mother and a good one. I believe it's the difference between a great preacher and a good one. I believe that in virtually every case, enthusiasm is the difference between being outstanding and being mediocre.

Psychologists have long known that if you act enthusiastic, you will soon be enthusiastic. In many companies, before they start the meeting, they sing a little song. Visitors attending those meetings say, "What's wrong with these people? They're jumping up and down, clapping their hands, and saying it's a great day. Are they out of their minds?" I don't know what else takes place at a lot of those meetings, but I can tell you that singing the song is 100 percent on target psychologically.

When you act enthusiastic, it's just a question of time before you will in fact be enthusiastic. I'm going to give you a formula. As I promised earlier, it's not going to cost any money, or take much time. It's not going to require any effort on your part, or at least it won't require as much effort as is required to run up and down a flight of stairs—and not nearly as much as required to do one of the modern dances or bring in the groceries. But if you'll follow this formula, two things will happen: you'll make more money, and you'll have more fun.

There is a catch, however: if you follow the formula I'm going to give you, you're going to be slightly embarrassed for a few minutes a day, especially if you have a mate. Are you willing to feel ridiculous for a few minutes a day to pick up an extra $15,000 or $20,000 a year?

When you set the alarm at night, you've decided, "I'm going to get up tomorrow morning at seven." When the alarm goes off, you don't decide again. You're going to get up; you've decided that. All you're going to decide now is *how* you're going to get up. You can get up as you've been doing it, or you can get up as if it's another magnificent day.

Tomorrow morning, when the alarm sounds, reverse the way you get out of bed. Now you're not going to get out of bed backwards. But when that alarm clock sounds off, many people rub their eyes, slap their face, and say, "Is it seven o'clock already? It seems like I just lay down. I've got a nine o'clock appointment, but that person isn't going to buy anything. No way."

Many people start every day as if it's going to be another yesterday, and they weren't overly excited about yesterday. But tomorrow morning, when that alarm clock sounds off, reach over, shut it off, sit straight up on the side of the bed, clap your hands and say, "Oh, boy, it's a magnificent day to get up and go to work!"

Now I want you to get the picture. There you are, on the side of the bed. Your hair is hanging down over your eyes. You're clapping your hands, you're acting like an eight-year-old child, and saying, "Oh, boy, it's a good day to get out and go to work!" If you live to be 168, you will never tell a bigger whopper than that. But you are up, and that is where you wanted to be. In addition, you have started to reach into your mind and take control of it.

Psychologically you're on sound ground, because when you sow an action, you reap a habit. When you sow a habit, you reap a character. When you sow a character, you reap a destiny.

This exercise is tremendously effective and fantastically beneficial. If you've got a big mirror right in front of you, you can see how totally ridiculous you look. It's a three-act comedy in full living color. I don't believe there's a normal human being in existence who can look at that ridiculous sight and not get hysterical.

Guess who you'll be laughing at? That's right, you'll be laughing at you. See if you can laugh at yourself. The surest sign of a lousy self-image is the fact that you cannot stand it if somebody else laughs at you, because you cannot laugh at yourself. You're psychologically healthy if you can sincerely laugh at yourself.

It will provide a double benefit if both husband and wife get up in the morning and do exactly the same practice. Now you've got a double comedy in living color. You're going to discover that you're going to be laughing with each other instead of laughing at each other. And does it ever make a tremendous difference!

Now you're up, so what do you do? You go into the bathroom and take a shower. While you're taking that shower, sing loud (unless there are small children asleep). And don't give me this old jazz about, "I can't carry a tune." Mitch Miller once wrote me a personal letter asking me not to even bother to sing along with him.

The tune is not the important thing. The fact that you are singing is the important thing. William James said, "We do not sing because we're happy. We are happy because we sing." Incidentally, this practice is scripturally sound, because it is written: "This is the day which the LORD hath made; we will rejoice and be glad in it" (Psalm 118:24).

You may be an enormously successful person: you've made an absolute fortune; you got your PhD; you are brilliantly educated. You may be middle-aged; maybe you're even a senior citizen. And I have the audacity to suggest that you get up and make like an eight-year-old child, singing and clapping your hands and all those ridiculous things!

You'd better believe I have the audacity to suggest you do that. If you resist, saying, "That doesn't apply to me," or "I never would do that," friend, be careful, because you badly need what I'm talking about.

When you put that action in, something is going to come out before the first day is over. As a matter of fact, you will find yourself snickering or smiling, thinking about the very idea: "Here I am, a successful, intelligent businessman or woman, sitting on the side of my bed, acting like an eight-year-old child!" Then you realize, "Who knows about it?"

Getting up like this is a good habit. Without exception, you must grab and hang onto good habits. Destructive habits grab you slowly, gradually, and easily over a long period of time until before you realize it, the destructive habit has got you. It doesn't matter whether the habit is alcoholism, obesity, profanity, promiscuity, drugs, or whatever. If it's a destructive habit, it sneaks up on you gradually and slowly. But when you have a good habit, you've got to grab it.

As I've mentioned already, jogging was a good habit for me. I had to force myself initially; later it got to be fun. Saving money is a good habit that you must force yourself to do. Tithing is a good habit; being courteous is a good habit. Initially, you will have to force yourself to do many things.

Then in the case of you fellows, when you go into the kitchen and there is breakfast on the table—I know you've probably had bacon, eggs, and grits every day for the last 187 days of your life. But this time, when you see the bacon, eggs, and grits on the table, slap the table and say, "Hon, you mean we've got bacon, eggs, and grits this morning? That's exactly what I was hoping you were going to have!" The shock value alone will be worth watching, I can guarantee you.

What are you doing with all of these activities? You are getting yourself into action. These are some of the greatest procrastination eliminators ever. And, as you know, most people tend to procrastinate over and over.

You've probably heard the story of Satan's sales meeting. He called all of his little devils together and said, "We've got Billy Graham and some of these other fellows going around the country, and they're doing too good a job. We're losing some of our finest potential recruits. Somebody's got to come up with a new plan to motivate them to come be with us in hell."

One little devil spoke up and said, "Satan, I've got an idea. Let's tempt the people with greed. Let's turn greed loose on them, and they will destroy themselves."

Satan said, "Boy, that's a good one."

Another devil said, "Let's tempt them with gambling. Let's even tell them that the way to do it is to start at a bingo game. Then we can easily move it on up with bets on football games and even state lotteries. Let's tempt them that way."

Satan said, "Boy, you hit that right on the head. That one's working well and exactly according to schedule, but we need something else."

Another one spoke up and said, "Let's tempt them with sex."

"Man," said Satan, "that's a good one. We've gotten more recruits with that one in the last twenty years than we'd gotten in the fifty years before that. But we've got to have something that's even more powerful and effective."

Finally, one little devil spoke up and said, "Satan, I've got the right plan right here. This will do it. This will work. Let's tell these people they should live good, clean, honorable, and noble lives. Let's tell them they should quit gambling and drinking. They should quit their immoral acts; they're not in their own best interest."

Satan spoke up and said, "Son, you are out of your mind. That's the craziest thing I ever heard of."

The little devil said, "No, wait a minute, Satan, you didn't let me finish. Let's tell them that they should quit all of those things and live a good, clean, moral life, but let's also tell them there's no hurry: tomorrow is soon enough to start."

Satan said, "That's it. That's the greatest recruiting tool that I have ever heard from anybody."

Step two on this four-step formula is to establish some symbols. America is full of symbols. On every street corner in every city, there is one. Some people call it a red light; some call it a stoplight; some call it a traffic light. But if you think about it, you know that it is in fact a go light. It's put there for the express purpose of making traffic go. If you don't believe this, watch: any time one of them goes off, you'll notice that traffic backs up for blocks. It's not because the stoplight is on, but because the go light is off. Why do people call them stoplights? They've heard others call them stoplights, so they just repeat it. Yet the average American spends twenty-seven hours a year in front of a go light, waiting on the right color.

In the future, when you pull up in front of a go light, say, "Hey, look at that! It's got my name on it. It's mine. It's put there so I can go faster and more smoothly and easily to my destination." Make it a positive sign.

I've got a good friend named Bernie Lofchick, whom I will discuss more later. He is so positive that he has never had a cold; once in a while he will catch a warm. He is so positive that he never talks about the weekend, because he figures that's negative. He calls it the "strong end."

I know what you're thinking: "Get up in the morning, clap your hands, talk about go lights, warms, and strong ends. Ziglar, is all of that necessary?"

No, it's not necessary. You can be mediocre without it. But do you want to be mediocre? Again, what's the commission on the sale that you *almost* make? What's the difference between barely making it and barely missing? Isn't it a word, a phrase, a thought, an idea, an attitude? It's a little here and a little there. I'm talking about the little things that make the big difference between you and Mr. or Mrs. Mediocrity.

Every time you're involved in a conversation, deliberately mention a traffic situation so that you can talk about go lights. The reason you're going to do it is you cannot say "go light" with a straight face if your life depends on it.

I don't expect you to get hysterical; it's not that funny. But the mind is an associating machine. The minute you say "go light," you are no longer where you were; you're alive and enthusiastic again, and you're having a good time. You're saying, "Old Zig sure was right about that," and that's the stuff that the right mental attitude is made of.

The third step in this formula is simply this: set your gyroscopes. Many years ago, on the old *Candid Camera* TV program, a woman had a suitcase out in the corridor of an office building. In it was a gyroscope set to go straight ahead. A man would be walking down the corridor, and the woman would say to him, "Sir, would you take my suitcase into my office? It's too heavy, and I can't pick it up."

The man would say, "Sure, I'll be delighted to." He'd reach down, pick the suitcase up, and start walking toward the office. When he tried to turn it into the office, he could turn all he wanted to, but that gyroscope was set to go straight.

Inside of every creature on the face of this earth is a built-in gyroscope. The duck does not fly south by choice. The duck flies south because God built into that duck something called self-preservation. When the cold weather starts, the duck invariably goes south, without directions. The young squirrel stores nuts for the winter. Even though he might be by himself, a thousand miles from any other squirrels, with no previous experience of cold weather, God has built something into that squirrel that says, "You must store your food for the winter, or you're going to starve." In every creature there's a built-in self-preservation gyroscope.

I've said it before, and I'll say it again: human beings were designed for accomplishment, engineered for success, and endowed with the seeds of greatness. I believe a loving God has put you here to succeed, to be happy, to be healthy, to accumulate, to do, to make a contribution in the game of life. I believe that a departure from those accomplishments is the result of failing to follow a set procedure, because we are designed to succeed.

If you go to the lakeshore and watch the sailing boats out there, you'll see that they're going in 360 different directions. The wind is only blowing in one direction, so how do you account for the fact that they're going in so many different directions? It's very simple. On the boat there's a human being, and the human being has set the sail. It's the set of the sail that determines the direction of the boat.

We're given the choice. No other creature on the face of this earth but man has been given the choice of setting the gyroscope to go exactly where they want to go.

These are the first three steps. To review them:

1. Get up enthusiastically in the morning.
2. Identify the positive signals in life.
3. Set your gyroscope.

Now I'm going to warn you right now that if you do these things, some people will look at you critically and say, "Hey, that gal is different," or "That guy is different." Of course, they will be right. You'll be so different that you'll be one of the five people out of the original 100 who will be getting the things out of life that they want instead of having to want the things they've got.

Remember that since the beginning of time there has never been a statue erected to a critic. Other people may even laugh at you, but it's only the little world and the little people who will be laughing. The little world laughed, but the big world gathered on the banks of the Hudson to watch Robert Fulton go steaming by. The little world laughed, but the big world was at Kitty Hawk when the Wright Brothers made the historic flight that launched humanity on the present era of accomplishment. The little world laughed, but the big world was tuned in when Alexander Graham Bell made that historic phone call.

Yes, that little world might laugh when you start your journey, but I can guarantee you that the big world is going to be right there at the finish line, cheering you as you cross it. Most importantly, what you get by reaching your destination will not be nearly as important as what you will become.

*   *   *

Have you already had lunch today? If so, do you plan to eat dinner this evening? That means that what you had for lunch was no good, right? No. What does it mean? It means that what you ate for lunch was for this afternoon, and what you're going to eat this evening is going to be for the rest of the night.

Most people eat food three times a day, on a schedule. But if I ask the same people, "When was the last time you regularly fed your mind?" they look at me and say, "What are you talking about?"

We get so involved in feeding our stomachs that if we ever miss a meal, we'll tell every friend and relative in sight: "I was so busy yesterday, I didn't even have time to eat lunch."

From your neck down, you're worth about $60 a week, yet we feed that part of our body three times a day. From the neck up, you're worth tens of thousands of dollars a year, yet most people feed that part of themselves occasionally, accidentally, or when it's convenient.

If anything, we should reverse the process, because if we feed our minds on schedule, we will never have to worry about feeding our stomachs. We will never have to worry about the roof over our heads or the footsteps of old age creeping up on us, because we're going to be beautifully prepared for all of those things.

Let's look at feeding the mind. It's interesting: the people who desperately need mental nourishment the most are the ones who resist it the most (which is, of course, the reason they need it the most).

These people look at things in reverse. For example, they will see somebody earning a large sum of money and say, "If I made that much, I guarantee I'd have a good attitude too." They think that they'd have got a good attitude because they're earning the money, but the reverse is obviously true. Those people are earning the money because they have a fantastic attitude.

As I've mentioned, when things are good, everybody's got a good attitude. But when things are bad, many people have a bad attitude. Again, we need to reverse that; we need to build this attitude foundation so that when things are good, your attitude is good; when things are bad, your attitude is still good, which means that soon things will be good.

Let's look a little deeper at the way the mind works. Everything that we learn, we learn consciously. But as long as you do something consciously, you're going to do it poorly.

A woman once mentioned that her daughter was playing the flute. She said, "She plays every single day, over and over." When this daughter first started playing the flute, I'll guarantee all of her friends and relatives avoided her. They will continue to avoid her until she has learned to play so well consciously that she moves it over into the subconscious mind, and she no longer even has to think about which note she's playing. She rattles it off without any difficulty.

If you learned to drive a car with a clutch, you remember the process: you would say to yourself, "Now mash the clutch, shift the gear, feed the accelerator, ease out on the clutch. Look out. Easy, easy." You were an absolute menace to society. You backed up over the curb, you ran over the street, and your instructor was saying, "Look out. Hit the brake. Turn it off. Do something."

You were dangerous because you were driving the car consciously. Later, you learned so well that you mashed the clutch, shifted the gear, fed the accelerator, and let out on the clutch while rolling down the window, lighting a cigarette, and talking to the other person in the car. You had moved the process from the conscious mind over to the subconscious mind.

Everything can be moved from the conscious mind into the subconscious mind, including courtesy, thoughtfulness, the right attitude, the right demonstration of affection to our mates. Even humor, positive thinking, the right mental attitude, and enthusiasm can be so completely moved from the conscious mind into the subconscious that we no longer have to think about them. We don't think about enthusiasm; we don't think about the right attitude; we don't think about courtesy; we don't think about smiling. All these things become a part of us.

This is not something that you're going to do in a twenty-four-hour period; you're not going to change a lifetime of habits that quickly. It might not even be easy. But it most assuredly, positively can be done.

You can even get to be like this old boy down home. There was a flash flood, and he was up on a rooftop. One of his neighbors came floating by and said, "John, this flood is just awful."

John said, "No, man. "It ain't so bad at all."

"What do you mean it ain't so bad? There goes your henhouse floating down the stream right now."

"Yeah, that's true. But don't you remember I started raising ducks six months ago? There they are, every one of them, just swimming around. Everything is going to be all right."

"Yeah, man, but look all this water. It's going to ruin your crops."

"No, it's not. The county agent told me a month ago that my crops were shot this year. And this land needed lots of water. This solved that problem, didn't it?"

"Yeah, but look: the waters are rising. First thing you know, they're going to be up to your windows."

"Boy, I sure hope so. You know, they're dirty and sure do need washing."

Maybe that's a joke, but many things that are said in jest are in fact truths. I believe that the Scriptures are accurate when they say we should thank God for everything. Regardless of what happens, if we react properly to a negative situation, an enormous amount of good comes from it. The year there was a gasoline shortage, 11,000 lives were saved as a direct result.

Let's look now at motivation. There are basically three kinds. The first is *fear motivation*. You tell your son or daughter, "If you're not in by eleven o'clock tonight, that's the last time this month you get the car." Or, "If you don't raise your grades, you're going to have your television viewing restricted."

Fear motivation says, "If you do that one more time, I'm going to go straight to the supervisor and tell him exactly what you've done." Fear motivation works for some people, but in most cases, the effect is short-range at best.

The second kind of motivation is *incentive motivation* or *carrot motivation*: "If you perform or produce, we're going to give you a trip to the Bahamas." "If you get three A's, we're going to give you a new stereo when you graduate."

As I've already stressed, employers want to pay their employees more money—universally, without exception. Why don't they? Because they do not run a benevolent institution. It's a profit-making venture (at least that's the reason they started). And you'd better hope they do make a profit, because if they don't, they're out of business, and maybe you're out of a job. Employers want to pay you more because they want you to produce more. When you produce more than you're worth, the reward will follow the action.

I'm certain you've seen the picture of the donkey pulling the cart. Right in front of the donkey is a carrot. This is incentive motivation, and it works if certain conditions are met: if the carrot is sweet enough, if the load is light enough, and if the donkey is hungry enough.

In short, if you want the reward, incentive motivation will work, but it won't work forever unless you let the donkey take a bite of the carrot. Otherwise, he's going to figure, "This is a con game. I'm never going to catch up to that carrot," and quit pulling altogether. The reward must be forthcoming eventually. You must let the donkey take a bite of the carrot.

You let the donkey take a bite of the carrot, and now you've got a brand-new problem, haven't you? The donkey is no longer hungry. Now you've got to shorten the stick, lighten the load, sweeten the carrot, and hope the donkey is still willing to pull. But the day comes when you can no longer lighten the load, shorten the stick, or sweeten the carrot because all the profit is now gone.

OK, now what are you going to do, Charlie Brown? The answer is amazingly simple: you change the donkey to a racehorse and make him want to run.

We call that the third kind of motivation, *internal habit pattern changes*. Two thousand years ago, Jesus Christ said, "Man can change." Every day of my life, I become more convinced that we, as individuals, can change. You've heard the old saying, "You can lead the horse to water, but you can't make him drink." But we can let him lick the salt block. If he licks that salt block, he is going to get thirsty enough that he is going to want to do something about his thirst, so in fact he will go out and drink the water.

We can dangle in front of you the rewards, or proper motivation, and let you see the benefits from it so that the reward is high and the results are beautiful. The change is so significant that you're going to say, "Hey, I believe that it's worth the effort," and then is when we go to work.

As I've mentioned, Dr. David McClelland at Harvard University completed a twenty-five-year study of the factors involved in success. He points out that you can change motivation by changing the way you think about yourself and your circumstances. That's really what this book is all about: changing the way you see yourself and your circumstances.

Dr. McClelland also discovered that motivation was significantly more important than many of the other factors in success. Let me give you some examples about changes that have taken place.

I believe these three following stories will firmly establish in your mind once and for all that regardless of what's happened in your past, if you really want to do something about yourself—if you want more rewards, more money, more friends, more peace of mind, more security, more happiness, more accomplishment, more of everything—you can.

Several years ago, I read a book entitled *The Rape of the Mind*. It was written by a Dutch psychiatrist named Joost A. Meerloo. In this book, he tells how during the Korean War, the North Koreans would take our young GI prisoners of war and subject them to brainwashing. Two communistic indoctrinators would go to work on a young GI, twenty or twenty-one years old. They'd start pumping their garbage in for ten to twelve hours. Then they would bring in two fresh indoctrinators, who would go on for ten or twelve hours more, then two more fresh ones, and so on.

Finally, after several days of this procedure—often after complete physical, mental, and emotional exhaustion—the young GI would throw in the towel and say, "All right." Although he had bitterly resisted, those lies were forced into his mind thousands upon thousands of times, so he ended up believing something that he had initially rejected. These prisoners started out fighting, but the power of the spoken word, repeated into their minds over and over, overcame their resistance.

There was one exception: those young GIs who had strong religious convictions. They were able to withstand the brainwashing. (Let me emphasize that Meerloo is not a religious man.)

If you read Isaiah 40:31, you'll know why. That verse says, "But they that wait upon the LORD shall renew their strength; they shall mount up with wings as eagles; they shall run, and not be weary; and they shall walk, and not faint." In the original Hebrew, the word for *renew* means *to change* or *exchange*. When you serve God, you change or exchange your strength for his. The young GIs could not resist, but when God enters the picture, you've got the eternal arithmetic that says that you plus God equals enough.

If these men fell victim to suggestion even though they resisted, then what about us in our everyday lives, when we don't give a thought to resisting anything? We float along in neutral and leave our minds open as a catch-all. We flip on the TV or radio or listen to a conversation without any thought of whether it's good, bad, or indifferent, or whether it's going to help us or hurt us. We just leave our minds open, and the garbage is dumped in.

Let me give you a positive example of what happens when we direct what flows into our mind. One of the most amazing stories I've ever read involves the late Shinichi Suzuki, a Japanese scientist who taught music to children.

Starting when they were six weeks old, he would take a cassette player and put it beside the crib. The baby would listen to the beautiful music for a month; the next month, he would play another tune; the next month, another tune. For two solid years, this is what happened to that baby.

Then he would give the baby a miniature violin, about one fifth regular size, and that child began to feel the instrument. At about two and a half, the mother of the child started taking violin lessons, with the child observing. When the child was about three years old, the child started taking the lessons. By the time it was five, it was playing beautiful music.

Suzuki once held a concert, with over fifteen hundred Japanese children, with an average age of less than eight. They were not playing "Twinkle, Twinkle, Little Star." They were playing Chopin and Beethoven and Vivaldi—the classics. According to Suzuki, virtually none of these children had any "natural musical ability." It was a learned skill.

The way babies learn to speak is very simple. They are around adults and older children who speak. This is exposure. In the second step, the baby tries to talk: the baby imitates language. When the baby comes out with a word resembling what somebody else has said, mother and dad call their friends and relatives and brag about it. What does that do for the baby? It provides the next step, which is encouragement. The baby goes around the house, repeating everything back and forth. Next, the baby starts improvising, tying the words together, and putting them into sentences and phrases. By the time the baby is three or four years old, they know a lot of words. That's the learning process.

One other example: a scientist was studying two tribes of American Indians. He noticed that neither of these tribes had a single individual who stuttered. He wondered if this was a coincidence or if this was characteristic of Indians. He did a study on every American Indian tribe living on reservations, and he could not find a single Indian that stuttered. Then he decided to do a study on Indian languages and dialects. When he had completed it, he understood why no Indians stuttered: because their languages and dialects did not have a word for *stutter*.

If there is no word for *stutter*, how could they stutter? They could not, because a word communicates a picture, and the individual takes that picture and completes it.

If, then, you were to change your vocabulary to remove the negatives and substitute the positive, what would happen? Take the word *hate* out of your vocabulary. Don't read it, don't see it, don't think it, don't say it. In its place, put *love*. Remove the word *prejudice* from your vocabulary, and in its place put *understanding*. Replace the word *negative* with *positive*. I wonder what the results would be.

In all, there are a hundred different words that you could change. In this way, you change your mental setting. Your mind acts on what you feed it. If we first reduce, then eliminate the negative input, it's just a question of time before we reduce and then virtually eliminate the negative output, because nothing could come out until it has first gone in. Nothing can come up until we have first planted it. Remember, we bring out the most recent crop that's been planted in our minds. So we stop planting and letting others plant the negative, and we put the positive in.

Many times, people say, "Zig, I'm busy. I'm running just to stay even right now. When am I going to have time to feed my mind, to read all of those books, and listen to all of those recordings?"

Let me pursue this one more step. The average professional spends hundreds, indeed thousands, of dollars a year on hair care, clothing, and transportation. After all this money has been spent, what have we got? A well-groomed, well-dressed, upwardly mobile professional. Now does it make sense to know what to say and do after you get to where you're going?

I'm going to suggest that we start feeding our minds with a proper mental diet. I'm going to start with listening to audio recordings. I do not personally know a self-made millionaire who does not regularly listen to audio recordings.

When do they listen? While they shave. While they apply makeup. While they boil the beans. While they clean the house. While they do 101 other things. They listen on the way to the office or to a sales call.

They listen at any time they don't have to pay attention to what they're doing.

Driving is a tremendously effective time for listening to audios. The University of California discovered that if you live in Los Angeles, over a three-year span, you can acquire the equivalent of two years of college education while in the car.

I can tell you with certainty that the astronauts listened to audio recordings while they were on the space platform circling the earth and on their way to the moon. The billionaire H. L. Hunt was still listening to daily recordings when he was past eighty years old. At one recent national convention, they had nineteen winners in a particular contest: seventeen of them, including the top eleven, listened to audio recordings every day.

I personally have in excess of 300 hours of audio material that I've accumulated over the years, and I never go anywhere by myself when I am not listening to these recordings.

By listening over and over, we fill our minds with inspiring material. Furthermore, you can never get the information on these recordings in one listening. A study at one major university showed that if you hear something just one time, two weeks later you will only remember 2 percent of what you've heard. If you listen for six consecutive days, two weeks later you will remember 62 percent of it. Infinitely more importantly, you will be more inclined to take action on what you have heard.

I have personally discovered that you need to listen to something about sixteen times in order to get the complete message. Even after you've heard it twenty or thirty or even forty or fifty times, you still respond emotionally to the message. And let me remind you that our thinking brain is only 10 percent as large as our feeling brain. We need to keep feeding in positive reinforcement so that we feel excited and motivated.

When I'm out of town, I always call my wife every night. I try to persuade her that saying, "I do" all those years ago was the smartest thing she ever said, and she tries to persuade me of the same thing. When I call her, I always tell her how much I love her, for two reasons. First of all, it's true.

Second, when I say, "I love you," I'm not educating her, but I am keeping the account open and up-to-date, and I'm keeping her enthused, inspired, and motivated. Why would I want to do that? I love her, and I want her to stay exactly like that.

I tell my wife that I love her not to educate her, but for the same reason you need to listen to the same recording over and over: we don't need to be told, but we do need to be reminded.

Nobody is smart enough to remember everything they know.

Many people believe that listening to inspirational audios or reading motivational books is excellent when you're down. I agree: they will pick you up. But often the best and most opportune time to listen or read is when you're at your peak, when you're riding high, when you're the most enthusiastic.

The reason is very simple: The first few times you listen up to a certain level of awareness. My friend Sandy Ragnar, who is one of the most enthusiastic and motivated people that I've ever seen, says, "A lot of times, people listen to something that brings them to one level of awareness. A month later, they hear the same thing again. Because they're at a higher level, it moves them up even further."

This is a very significant point. Frequently, when you are down, you reject some of the most productive ideas as not being applicable to you. But when you're riding high and the ideas are presented forcefully and enthusiastically to your subconscious mind, you say, "That's exactly what I've been looking for." You accept an idea that you had previously rejected when you were a little bit lower.

Certainly inspirational books and recordings can serve as stepping stones to get you out of the dumps. But they can also serve as a stepladder to get you off mediocrity row, out of the crowd at the bottom, or even as an unencumbered escalator to take you all the way to the top.

Because this is a good habit, like getting up in the morning, you've got to remind yourself to do it. You've got to write yourself little notes; you've got to force yourself into taking action. As I've already mentioned, when

I set the goal of losing thirty-seven pounds, many times when the alarm clock would sound off, I fussed about it, say, "I don't want to get up," but then I would look down at that forty-one-inch waistline. I would say to myself, "Ziglar, do you want to look like you, or do you want to look like that picture hanging in the bathroom mirror?" I didn't want to look like me, so out of bed I'd get. After I forced myself to do this for a while, one day I found out I was having fun doing it.

The four steps are very simple:

1. Get up enthusiastically in the morning.
2. Establish positive symbols.
3. Set your gyroscope.
4. Feed your mind on a regular basis.

10

The Force of Habits

At this point, we're going to look at habits. Good habits will take you to the top; destructive habits will chain you to the bottom.

I want to take an in-depth look at habits, and I want you to follow me carefully, because little information has ever been passed out concerning the habits that we must acquire if we're going to succeed in the game of life.

First of all, when you choose the habit, you choose the end result. How do you get bad habits? If you smoke, you will remember that the first time you put a cigarette in your mouth, your entire body rebelled and said, "No, no, no." But you said, "Oh, yes, you are," and you started forcing that cigarette in your mouth. All your friends, neighbors, and relatives smoke, so you've got to do it too.

The body adjusted: "All right. I'll do it. But I'm not going to like it." Later, you learned how to smoke. Remember how proud you were the first time you could blow smoke through your nose? Once you were a big boy or girl, you could blow a smoke ring. And weren't you something when you could blow a smoke ring through a smoke ring? The day came when you could casually talk and let the smoke leak out of your mouth at the same time without any thought. You could inhale casually and flip the ashes off to let everybody know you were an old-timer at this gig. You know what happened: you were accepted by your peer group.

You were one of the gang, but you still wouldn't admit you had the habit. Your mother or daddy would say, "Hey, you'd better quit that. You're going to end up getting the habit." You'd say, "Oh, not me. I'm just playing with it. I can quit anytime I want to. As a matter of fact, I've already quit nine times."

When I see kids in bowling alleys, they seem to be smoking more than any other players; I don't know why. But when I go to a bowling alley and see an eight- or nine- or ten-year-old child smoking, it's almost more than I can stand. I want to sit them down, put them across my knees, and warm their bottoms, as their mother and daddy should have done, and give them a nice, long lecture about what will happen if they continue. Obviously, I don't do that. But as I watch these kids, I turn the calendar forward, and I know what's going to happen to them. I've never talked to a smoker in my life who wouldn't give anything in this world if they had never acquired the habit.

You know the final stage of smoking: you really don't get the habit; the habit gets you. I've seen 200-pound men reduced to a quivering mess by a cigarette that weighed less than one-third of an ounce. They can't wait. They would mortgage their souls for one more cigarette, admitting that that little piece of tobacco is more powerful than they are. You're playing with something pretty dangerous when you get into a habit like that.

Nobody starts out to become obese, but if you gain one ounce a day, you're gaining twenty-three pounds per year. I'm talking about a bite here and a bite there. Similarly, nobody starts out to become a drug addict. I've done a great deal of work in the drug war, but I've never talked to a young-ster on pot who said, "I'm just fooling with this now, but this is October. By December, I'm going to move up to hashish. By next May, I'm going to be on speed. By next October, I'm going to be mainlining heroin." I have never talked to anyone who had that as their objective. They always say, "I'm too smart for that. I'm never going to get involved."

I've never talked to an alcoholic who said that when they were young and started to drink, they were setting out to become alcoholics. Nobody sets out to destroy themselves. Prostitutes do not become prostitutes by choice or design. Over a period of time, it was a slip here and a slip there, and the self-image was destroyed. The next thing we know, we've got real problems.

I've never talked to one hard-core drug addict who did not start with marijuana, and I've talked to lots of them. The day we legalize marijuana, we've got the most serious problem this country has ever been confronted with. We don't have all of the evidence as yet as far as marijuana is concerned. But this we do know: it affects judgment. It multiplies the incidence of birth defects nearly tenfold. It diminishes sex drive. It removes some of our inhibitions and enables us to do things that ordinarily we would not do. We know that marijuana destroys cells, and we know that it creates apathy.

Every single bad habit starts slowly and gradually. Kids start with marijuana. And it's never an underworld character who makes a new convert; it's always a close friend or relative. It lessens the guilt in their mind if they can get somebody that they respect to join them in this illicit activity. Then some bright young man or girl in the crowd says, "Listen, if you think this is fun, you haven't tried anything until you've tried speed or LSD or hashish." I'll lay you $11 to a nickel that the same source that supplied the marijuana will supply the harder drug. One thing leads to another.

At first, the youngster who started with marijuana doesn't have to do anything but get a few pennies out of their allowance, and that supplies it. As they smoke more heavily, they've got to take a little money out of mom's change purse. As they get into speed or hashish or LSD, they've got to start taking a few items from around the house. A little later, they start stealing from a local store and selling it to a fence. As they move up into heroin, they have to steal almost on a full-time basis to supply the habit. Pretty soon, they cannot even do that. The girls very frequently turn to prostitution and the boys to procuring. Even that eventually does not satisfy the habit, which runs up to several hundred dollars a day. Now that nice young boy or girl who had a little joint two years earlier becomes a drug pusher. And when you have a new drug pusher, you've got to get new prospects, because if the new person tries to sell to established customers, the drug pusher who's already established will slit their throat.

That's the reason that marijuana is so deadly. My organization advocates the death penalty for a convicted pusher of hard narcotics. Is that hard? I don't think you would agree that it's too hard if you had ever seen a fourteen-year-old prostitute with scabs on her. I don't think you would say it if you ever heard a fifteen-year-old screaming, "Make me like I was."

A confirmed addict will do anything to get a fix, including murder and selling their own wives or sisters as prostitutes. They might do anything while on a trip, including killing their best friend and eating their heart (there is one documented case when this actually happened).

Every destructive habit starts slowly and gradually speeds up. Profanity starts with one word and then two words. A lot of people who spout profanity are not even aware of some of the things that they are saying. Promiscuity starts the same way. The person who's late to work every day got in the habit of doing that by starting a little bit; then it picks up. The alarm clock goes off, and they turn it off to catch two more winks. Later, they say that the alarm clock didn't go off this morning.

Once my mother and I were riding from Columbia, South Carolina, to Charleston. My mother finished fifth grade as far as formal education is concerned, but she graduated magna cum laude from the university of life. When my children came along, she used to say to me, "Son, your children more attention pay, to what you do than what you say."

On this particular trip, I asked my mother about one of my classmates, who had graduated with me from high school. She lowered her voice and leaned over to tell me in a whisper, because it was so awful. She said, "Son, he's become the worst kind of a drinker."

I facetiously said, "Well, mama, what is the worst kind of a drinker?"

"Why son, he will buy a bottle, and he'll take it home, and he'll close the doors. And there, in the privacy of his own home, he will take one drink right by himself, and that's all he ever takes."

"Mama, that's the worst kind of a drinker? How in the world do you figure that?"

"Well, son, you think about it. If he were a sot drunk in the gutter, who would he inspire to drink? The way he does it, he denies his family nothing. He never gets out of the way. He never abuses his wife, never denies his family anything because of his drinking. He makes it sophisticated. The children look and say, 'Dad's a hard worker. He's a good provider. Certainly there is nothing wrong with him taking an occasional drink. When I grow up, I want to be just like Dad.'"

Every bad habit starts that way. You think I exaggerate. In France, they have the highest rate of alcoholism in the world. By coincidence, they have also the highest rate of wine consumption in the world. They start with just a little bit of alcohol. You think it was an accident?

Let's go down to Chile. They happen to have the second highest rate of wine consumption in the world. Would you believe they also have the second highest rate of alcoholism in the world?

I think you'll agree with me, regardless of your religious persuasion, that the Catholic priest is one of the most dedicated, conscientious, sincere, hardworking, best-educated individuals on the face of this earth. They dedicate their lives to the priesthood. The Catholic church does not frown on the social drink, although they obviously frown on alcoholism and drunkenness. These dedicated priests go to cocktail parties where they're expected to have a cocktail. As a result, one out of ten becomes an alcoholic.

We now know that one person out of sixteen who takes an occasional drink will become an alcoholic, yet nobody starts out to become one. The Surgeon General of the United States requires cigarette manufacturers to put warnings on cigarette packs. I don't know why they don't do the same thing on bottles of alcohol, because comparing the dangers of smoking to the dangers of alcohol is like comparing a pea shooter to a fifty-caliber machine gun.

A lot of Americans were concerned about the Vietnam war. We lost 56,000 lives. During the same period, drunken drivers on the highway alone killed in excess of 500,000 people. This year, every one of the thousands who will die on the highway as a result of drunk driving will be killed by someone who started with one drink.

Now what are we going to do about bad habits? First of all, the best thing is never to start them. You might say, "That's smart, but I've already started them. Now what am I going to do?" Take a good look at the end result. Don't ever even get curious.

Something that is moral or immoral can be caught as well as taught. You're thrown into a social situation that you might originally abhor, such as wife swapping. You say, "Oh, I didn't want any of that." It repels you; it's repugnant to you. You can't understand it. But if you associate with these people, you'll learn that the most beautiful word is *tolerance*.

That's for the birds. Some things should never be tolerated. Tolerance is good only as it applies to certain things. At first, we accept things, then we give tacit approval, and then we get involved. You can't know how many addicts have told me, "That's exactly what happened to me."

Professor Alexander Becker at Yale University said that pornography produces a moral atmosphere, and the moral atmosphere is the ultimate regulator of conduct. If something can be shown, society begins to think that it is doable, and when they think it's doable, they begin to participate.

If you want to avoid or stop bad habits, change your associations. Get with the right crowd, because you do become part of what you're around. Solomon was the most brilliant man who ever lived, blessed beyond belief, and given all the money imaginable. And the Lord said, "Solomon, don't mess with those heathen women. They worship idols." Solomon married some. He worshiped idols. The Lord told Samson, "Keep your hair." Delilah smooth-talked him into a haircut, and he ended up as a blind slave. The wisest and the strongest fall.

We become desensitized to certain things. When you associate with something long enough, you're no longer aware of it. People who live in paper mill towns are soon unaware of the odor. You become desensitized to the actual situation.

These habits are tough to eliminate, but one way to eliminate them is to substitute. I like Alcoholics Anonymous, because a person who goes into that program is forced to accept two things at the very beginning. First of all, they are forced to accept that *they* became alcoholics; it wasn't because their mother was scared by a runaway horse or the second-grade teacher slapped them on the third day of school, but because they drank too much booze. Second, they have to accept the fact there is nothing they can do about it. They must go to a higher authority. They turn the problem over to Almighty God. They substitute a positive for a negative. They associate with people who get up and say, "I did it, and you can too. I did it and you can too." They get hope and encouragement, and they substitute loving and caring friends for drunken friends from the past.

That's exactly what happens at Weight Watchers, TOPS (Take Off Pounds Sensibly), and other weight-loss associations. People have a problem. They come and they see other people who have whipped it, and they say, "If he or she can, I can whip identically the same problem." We need to associate with the right crowd.

Bad habits are enormously tough to get rid of. In Lexington, Kentucky, the federal government spent millions of dollars for a drug rehabilitation center for heroin addicts, and they spent millions of dollars more working with these addicts. The facility had the best medical and psychiatric brains and the most restorative or curative drugs in the country. The net result was that less than 3 percent of the addicts who went through the Lexington facility were returned to a productive life. The results were so bad that the federal government closed it down.

I was startled to read that only 3 percent of the alcoholics, under the best medical and psychiatric treatment, are restored to normalcy. The doctors themselves will say that 2 percent would have quit drinking on their own, so that gives them 1 percent.

There is a better way. David Wilkerson wrote a book entitled *The Cross and the Switchblade*. He was heavily involved in the drug rehabilitation program. His organization has a success rate of over 80–85 percent. They don't use any drugs; in many cases, they have no withdrawal symptoms. Their cure is Jesus Christ.

Many members of the medical community and even the nonbelieving community are now saying, "If the results are that good, maybe we ought to look at it."

I was out in Albuquerque, New Mexico, and became acquainted with an organization called DARE: Drug Addicts Rehabilitation Enterprises. It was in an old Catholic school, abandoned because they didn't think it was serviceable any longer. You drove into the village and saw a little sign that said their village population consisted of one family.

I walked through the village. I met pimps and prostitutes, robbers and murderers and forgers. I met every kind of humanity from the dregs that you can possibly imagine. Yet as you looked at these young people (and most of them were young), you were no longer able to distinguish that they had a problem. They were smiling, enthusiastic, friendly, and cheerful.

I was told that 85 percent of the village consists of the addicts that come in. That's the one thing they all have in common: they're all drug addicts, most of them hard-core, who have done everything they could to quit but had been unsuccessful. Of those who stay at the village for forty-eight hours, approximately 85 percent are restored to complete health—again, without drugs, without medication, without psychiatric help. Their only cure is Jesus Christ.

Regardless of your belief, let me ask you a very simple question. Let's say you had a fatal disease. (And drug addiction is fatal. Sometimes it takes years, but it eventually gets you unless something is done about it.) You go to two doctors, both surgeons. One says, "If I operate, I give you a 3 percent chance of recovery." The other one says, "If you come to me, I give you an

85 percent chance of recovery." Now you and I both know which doctor you would choose, don't we?

If you want to get rid of your habit, feed your mind with the good, the clean, the pure, the powerful, the positive. Listen to inspiring recordings and read motivational books. Follow the steps that I've outlined, and you definitely can free yourself. If you have none of these habits, you've got something else that you need to pray and thank God for.

Suppose you were an employer, and you were looking for an employee. What kind of employee would you want? Suppose you could order this employee out of a catalog, and the order would be filled according to your exact specifications.

Would you want this employee to be completely dependable, honest, and always on the job? Would you want this employee to be willing to follow instructions? Would you want them to be brilliant, capable, pleasant, agreeable, and more than willing to work for room and board on a lifetime contract? I'll bet you this is the kind of an employee you would like to have.

Suppose you had such an employee; how would you treat him? The employee's performance depends entirely upon the way you treat him. If you are courteous and thoughtful, he will work for you long and hard. But if you're rude and inconsiderate, he'll be stubborn and rebellious. If you brag about him and tell him he is a smart fellow, he will do everything in his power to please you; he will perform brilliantly. But if you call him lazy, stupid, or irresponsible, he will rebel. He'll get so upset that he would foul up a two-car parade. Tell him that you love him and respect him, and he'll stay up all night solving your problem. But if you hate him and tell him you don't love him, he will become so frustrated that he won't do anything right.

If such an employee showed up at your door, would you hire him? That's a silly question, of course. But after you hired him, how would you treat him? We both know the answer to that one, don't we—or do we?

I forgot to tell you that this dream employee is easily influenced by the people around him. If he's around negative, garbage dump thinkers, in time he too will become a negative, garbage dump thinker. But if you surround him with positive people, he's going to be a positive talker and a positive doer.

I bet you've just decided to surround this dream employee with positive people. You've decided to create an environment for him that's going to be pleasant and agreeable so that you will get the absolute most out of him. You've got everything to gain by giving him this kind of an environment. You would plan on playing this one smart now, wouldn't you?

However, the chances are extremely good that you would abuse this dream employee. I say this because of the poverty that exists in millions of lives. Most people do abuse and misuse this fantastic employee, which is in reality your subconscious mind. It will perform exactly like the dream employee I've been describing.

Honestly, how have you been treating this prized employee, your subconscious mind, who will do exactly as you command, regardless of whether the instructions are positive or negative? It will bring out what you want. It will perform as you instruct. It will also do what you *don't* want it to do, although it will still act according to the instructions you have given it.

Charles Dennis Jones was undoubtedly a giant. Those who had seen what he did knew that he had to be a giant, because they had seen a truck go off the road, hit a tree, and turn over on its side, and a small fire started to burn. They called a wrecker, but they knew that the wrecker could not get there before the fire was too big, and the person inside would be burned to death.

All of a sudden, Charles Dennis Jones appeared. He walked over to the truck. He grabbed the door and started to pull. The pressure he exerted was so enormous that his shirtsleeves burst. After tremendous effort, he was able to open the door and reached in. The man inside had his leg wrapped around the clutch. With his bare hands, Charles Dennis Jones pulled the clutch out, snuffed out the flames, and rescued the man.

As he was leaving, somebody stopped him and said, "Why did you do this?" Charles Dennis Jones, a black man, six feet tall, weighing about 190 pounds, simply said, "I hate fire." Six months earlier, he had stood helplessly by and watched his small daughter burned to death. That was why he was able to do this feat.

Many times, you've been driving down the street, thinking about nothing in particular, and all of a sudden, boom! You say, "Oh, boy. That's it. Why in the world did I not think about that before? That's exactly the idea that I have been needing." I think every human being has had that experience.

A thirty-seven-year-old woman picked up a 3,600-pound car off her child because it had fallen on him. She was a slender woman, but she reached down and without a thought, without hesitation, picked up 3,600 pounds.

This woman, Charles Dennis Jones, and you driving down the street were all doing exactly the same thing: you were using your subconscious mind. You were doing it instinctively and automatically without any thought.

For generations, humans have dreamed of using the subconscious mind on a regular and deliberate basis in order to harness some of its enormous power. Let's see how the subconscious mind works, how it relates to the conscious mind, and how we can put it to work for us.

The conscious mind is the calculating, thinking, reasoning portion of your mind. It has the capacity to accept or reject anything it is presented. The subconscious mind, on the other hand, has a perfect memory. It never sleeps. It neither analyzes nor rejects any information, but accepts a command or instruction and fills the order just as surely as a typewriter will type the key you hit. It has unlimited power potential and storage capacity, so what you let go into it is terribly important.

You have probably seen some demonstrations of the power of hypnosis, which deals with the subconscious mind. I personally know Dr. Michael Dean, who teaches at the University of California, and who also is a nightclub performer. I've seen him hypnotize people and stretch a small woman between two chairs. He weighs over 200 pounds, but he would stand on the woman.

Does hypnosis increase strength? It might, but we don't think so. Rather it removes the barriers. Instead of thinking negative—"I can't do it"—those barriers are removed, uncovering the strength that is there.

Let me give you a practical, everyday example of what I'm talking about. Have you ever gone into an office and seen a desk that's piled high with papers?

You and the owner of the desk both smiled at the same time, and you said, "You can always tell a busy man," or "You can always tell a busy woman." Everybody grinned and snickered.

You can also tell something else about that "busy" individual. You can tell a lot about their income. Almost without exception, if the person is making a high income, the top of that desk is as clean as a whistle. If the desk is piled high, their earned income is, almost without exception, comparatively low.

Have you ever been working on something on your desk, and all of a sudden, out of the clear blue sky, have you reached over to another portion of the desk, gotten another piece of paper, and started working on that? Your vision picked up what was on the other side of the desk. That means you were not giving the project at hand every bit of your concentration. As a result, you were scattering your power, reducing it enormously.

Researchers took a college student and gave him a newspaper. They highlighted three paragraphs in the center and said, "Memorize those." He worked on it. They said, "OK, quote it to us." He only missed one or two words.

Then they said, "What else did you see on that page?" and he said, "Zero. I didn't see anything." Then they hypnotized the student. Not only did he give those three paragraphs perfectly, but he also quoted much of the rest of the page.

The reason is very simple: you don't look just straight ahead. If this were not so, you'd be a menace to yourself and society. You couldn't drive a car or walk down the street; you couldn't do anything. You have to have peripheral vision. But when you are picking up things off the desk with your eyes, you're dissipating your power of concentration.

This boils down to a simple procedure. If you don't learn anything else from this book, this one idea will save you time and make you money. Remove every single thing from your desk and put it in a drawer. Get it completely out of sight, then reach in, take one thing out at a time, work on it, dispense with it, and go to the next one. You will be 25 percent faster and considerably more effective. When you finish the day, instead of leaving something you've got to come back to, you are leaving a task that is completed. The psychological impact is tremendous. The subconscious mind gives you a much better response if you treat it that way: you perform much more effectively.

Most people go through life hypnotizing themselves into the negatives. They hypnotize themselves not to get the things they want, partly because, as I mentioned earlier, we live in a negative society. Never go to sleep at night with your radio on, because some of these programs are pretty wild. They will enter the mind, and you will find yourself instinctively agreeing with them, because the subconscious mind never, never sleeps. That's why some minds that are open should be closed for repairs.

Let me give you an example of how to work with the subconscious. We had a daughter that had a bedwetting problem. To correct it, we used to talk to her at night after she went to sleep. We would sit down by her and say, "You are such a beautiful child. Everybody loves you because you're so happy, you're so pleasant, you're so cheerful. You are such a marvelous little girl, because you always sleep in a warm, dry bed. As a matter of fact, you will sleep only in a warm, dry bed. If you should need to use the bathroom, you will wake up."

The first time I did this, I played a little dirty. In my family, I have always been the light sleeper. If any of the children were to awaken at night, they would always call me, because I instantly awoke; my wife outsmarted me for years by never hearing a thing. This particular night, I said to my daughter, "If you should awaken during the night, you will call your mother."

Around 1:30 a.m. I heard loud and clear, "Mommy." I was so tickled, I got up and took my daughter to the bathroom, but I always gave the instructions positively.

One of our girls was having difficulty with a spelling assignment. After she had gone to sleep, we sat by her bed and spelled the words over and over. The next day, she made 100 on the test.

How can we use the subconscious mind deliberately and regularly? First, know that everything you've ever learned, ever smelled, ever felt, tasted, touched, or even thought has become a permanent part of your subconscious mind. Second, the subconscious mind responds to stimuli rather than pressure. You stimulate it by listening to new educational and motivational material. Here's the exciting thing: the more new, exciting material you put into the mind, the more usable the material that is already there becomes.

Third, you can fool the subconscious mind, so be selective. That's one of the dangers of hypnosis. I've heard many times that you will not do anything under hypnosis that is against your moral fiber. That's not necessarily true, because the hypnotist could, for example, convince you that you were married to him. You might be against murder, but a hypnotist could say, "Why don't you take this water pistol and squirt water on him?" Except that it's not a water pistol.

You must not toy with an amateur hypnotist. It's dangerous. Doctors and dentists use clinical hypnotism for minor procedures, and it's used by some psychologists and psychiatrists. That's a different ball game. Don't foul up your mind and your life with an amateur who's playing parlor games. It's easy to put somebody under hypnosis. It's an entirely different matter to bring them out of it properly. Don't deal with an amateur.

Fourth, many people say, don't take your problems to bed with you. That's the most foolish advice that you've ever been given, because the bed is the place to solve your problem. Take your problem to bed with you.

If you have the extra advantage of believing in Almighty God, you can circumvent this part of the instruction. If you don't have this advantage, here's the instruction that you give your subconscious mind: As you lie down to sleep, you've mulled over the problem, you've thought about the factors involved, and you've weighed all the possibilities. You've gotten all of the data relevant to the problem. As you lie down, say to yourself, "Now, subconscious mind, you know what the problem is. You know all the information we have to solve the problem. I'm absolutely confident that when I wake up tomorrow morning, you will have the solution to the problem for me. I'm going to get a good night's sleep. You stay up and solve the problem, and sometime tomorrow, I will expect from you the answer." It's astonishing, the number of times this will happen.

Now I happen to be privileged to have a beautiful swimming pool. Late at night, particularly in cool weather, when I have been wrestling with something and can't solve it, I get into my swimming pool, which fortunately is heated. I have come to relate to that swimming pool as a place to solve problems; you need a problem-solving place. The answer often comes in a matter of minutes.

Step number five to using your subconscious mind: expect good things to happen. When you give your subconscious mind that instruction, expect it to happen, and then you will live in an area of expectancy. The next day, you're going to be amazed at the good things that do happen.

Step number six to using your subconscious mind: put a pencil and paper by your bed. Many times, when you're wrestling with a problem, you'll wake up in the middle of the night. You will think you've been dreaming, but you'll have the answer. Sometimes it's so vivid that you will say, "I'm excited about the answer! There's no way I'll ever forget this." But if you go back to sleep, you have just committed a cardinal sin, because often the next day you will completely forget. Hop up, write it down, and you'll sleep much better. If you do that, you will get an awful lot of answers. This is the way to use your subconscious mind.

11

Right Work

This chapter is about work. Actually, there is only so much you can say about work. I believe that if you have the right mental attitude, your goals are set, and you have the right kind of image about yourself, no one is going to have to say to you, "It's time to go to work." In most cases, they're going to have to tell you when to stop.

Somebody once said that doing nothing is the most tiresome job in the world, because you can't stop and rest (and how true that is!). Another wise man said that if you really want to kill time, just work it to death.

In this chapter, we have four objectives:

1. To sell the idea that there ain't no free lunch.
2. To clarify the difference between paying a price and enjoying a price.
3. To introduce you to a new attitude toward your job or profession.
4. To explain why you must put something in life before you can get anything out of life.

A king once called all of his wise men together and said, "I want you to go out and compile for me the wisdom of the ages. I want you to put it in book form so we can leave it to posterity."

The wise men went out and worked a long period of time. They came back with twelve huge volumes.

The king said, "That's tremendous. I'm confident that this is the wisdom of the ages, but it is so lengthy that nobody will read it. You must condense it."

The wise men went out and worked a long time. They came back with one volume. Again, the wise old king said, "It's too lengthy. You must condense it."

The wise men went out and worked again. They came back with a chapter, then a page, then a paragraph, and finally a sentence. When the wise old king saw it, he said, "That's it. That is the wisdom of the ages. As soon as all men everywhere know this, our problems will be solved." The sentence simply said, "There ain't no free lunch."

I'm convinced beyond any reasonable doubt that there ain't no free lunch: you cannot get something for nothing. Since I've been a little boy, I have been told by my elders and even by my peers that you can't get something for nothing: you've got to do your part. You've got to work; you've got to make a contribution.

A psychiatrist in Atlanta interviewed over a hundred young people at the ages of approximately twenty to twenty-one who wanted careers in music. He would ask, "Do you want to take a course in music?"

"No."

"Do you want to play a musical instrument?"

"No, I just want a career in music."

"A career in music doing what?"

"I just want to listen to music."

Can you believe it? These young people wanted to make a career of listening to somebody else make music. They wanted to sit there and be the recipient: "Here I am, world. Fill me full of good music. All I want to do is listen. I don't want to make any effort. I don't want to make any contribution."

It's part of a something-for-nothing philosophy that I guarantee you has never worked and never will. We've got to work. Education will cover a lot of ground, but it will not cover that.

Isn't it amazing, the number of people who show up for work every day but avoid it like the plague? If you expect to occupy your place in the sun, you've got to expect some blisters.

Yes, work is the price you pay to travel the highway of success.

Dr. H. M. Greenberg, a New Jersey psychologist, did a psychological evaluation of 186,000 people over a period of years. He discovered that over 80 percent of them went to work every day to a job that they did not like. Is it any wonder that we often have second-rate performances and third-rate merchandise?

People today often respond negatively. If somebody asks, "How are you doing?" the response is invariably, "Since I get off in an hour, I'm doing well," or "Since it's Friday, not too bad," or "Since this is the last week I've got to work on this job, everything is all right." It's amazing, the number of negatives that come out.

One night I was in Minneapolis on my way to Winnipeg, and I stopped at customs. I saw a little gal there, and I said, "How are you doing?"

"Since I'm off in an hour, not so bad; otherwise, bad."

"I can't believe you said that," I told her. "You're young, you're pretty, you're employed, you're healthy, and you're working in America, so you've got an opportunity to go wherever you want to go and do whatever you want to do. Now that you've thought about it, you're feeling great, aren't you?"

"You know what?" she said. "I hadn't thought about it, but now that you mention it, everything is much better than I thought."

It's astonishing, how we get in the habit of replying in the negative about work. It's almost as if it were a badge of honor to say, "I don't want to work," or "I don't like this," yet it borders on the ridiculous. We need to change our attitude towards our work.

As I've already emphasized, you do not pay the price for success. Look at a failure in life, and you'll understand that you don't pay the price for success; you pay the price for failure. Consider all benefits, the excitement, the joy, the glory, and the motivation that goes with success, and you know you enjoy the price of success.

One time when the famous French painter Pierre-Auguste Renoir was working on a painting, his arthritis was killing him, and every brushstroke was excruciating. He was obviously under great stress, and his face grew distorted. His good friend Henri Matisse, another great painter, asked him, "Why do you do it?" Renoir smiled and said, "The pain passes, but the beauty remains."

If we look at the end result, we can give glory, honor, and dignity to the work we're doing.

Charles Kettering, before he became a General Motors executive and founded the Delco Company, was the foreman of a company of men digging holes for a telephone company. One day, a hobo passed by as they were having lunch and asked for something to eat. Kettering got up from the site lunch, took the man down to a restaurant, and fed him a delicious meal. When the meal was over, he said to him, "How would you like to have a good job, which would enable you to eat delicious meals like this all the time?"

The hobo, thinking that since he had gotten a good free lunch, decided that the least he could do was express his appreciation by doing some work in exchange.

Kettering took the hobo to a spot and gave him the equipment to start digging the hole, and the hobo went to work. After about thirty minutes, Kettering came back and found that the hobo hadn't dug much of a hole. The ground was a jagged mess. Blisters were already on the hobo's hands, and he was sweating heavily.

Kettering said to the man, "Here is the way you do it. Watch what Joe is doing over here." Joe was the best hole digger they had, and he had dug a hole straight down. Kettering pointed out that it was perpendicular and smooth all the way around. It was an absolute work of art.

Kettering said, "Here is all you have to do." He showed the man how to wield the pick, round the edges, smooth off the hole, and make it perpendicular. He showed the hobo the beauty of digging a simple hole in the ground.

The hobo stayed. As a matter of fact, he became so good that he dug holes even better than Joe did. Later, they made him the foreman of the crew. One day, he said to Kettering, "You were the first person ever to tell me that work could be fun. If someone had told me that doing good work could be fun, I would never have been a bum."

Work gives us more than our living. It gives us our very life. If you show up for work eight hours a day, you're honest, sincere, and conscientious, and do your job for eight full hours, and the boss gives you your paycheck, you are exactly even. You hired yourself out, he paid you, you got what you came for, and you delivered what he hired you for; now everybody's even.

Under those circumstances, you do not deserve a raise. If you want a raise, it's what you do extra that will get it for you—the extra enthusiasm, the extra effort, the extra few minutes here and there.

Lou Scott says amen to this. Lou is the executive vice president of an organization called Management Recruiters International, the largest bureau for recruiting executive personnel in the country. During one recession, Lou told me, "Zig, we have no difficulty placing the people who always do the little bit of extra. They pay you to work forty hours. When you do that, then the average guy either quits or quits competing. It's easy to succeed, get a raise, and move ahead, when your competition has either quit or quit trying. We never have any difficulty placing the man or the woman who's willing to do the extra."

The Bible says, "If any would not work, neither should he eat" (2 Thessalonians 3:10). Out on the California coast, there was a cannery. The fishing boats would bring their catch in, and the cannery would can the fish and throw away the waste. They had no disposal problem, because the gulls were thousands in number, and they would act as scavengers. The gulls simply cleared up the fish, no problem.

Eventually, modern technology moved in, and the cannery started using all of the parts of the fish. Soon there was no waste. The gulls, over several generations, had never had to work for a living. The fish had been there; the gulls had had a free lunch right in front of them. Now they started starving to death.

Finally, they brought in some gulls from another area who had had to fish and work for a living. The new gulls taught the old gulls how to fish by example, and pretty soon all of the starving gulls started eating again.

Many times people say, "If somebody would just pay all my bills, and give me a start in life, I could climb the highest mountain. I could go anywhere; I could do anything. There's no limit to what I could do if somebody would come along and give me a start."

Dollars don't do it. In the 1950s, television quiz shows gave winners tens of thousands of dollars, even as much as $250,000. Several years later, researchers talked to the people who had had these huge amounts dropped in their lap. Not a single one had one single dime more than they had had before that money was dropped right in their laps. There ain't no free lunch.

There are three things that are hard to do. One is to climb a fence that's leaning toward you. Another is to kiss a girl that's leaning away from you. The third is to help people who do not really want to be helped. A person has to want to do their part.

If you want to create a cripple, give him a pair of crutches. Many assistance programs simply give out fish. When you give someone a fish, you feed him for the day. We need to concentrate on teaching the individual to fish. Then you feed that individual for life. When you eliminate the necessity for independence and standing on your own two feet, when you embrace a something-for-nothing philosophy—the world owes you a living—you're heading for difficulty.

Then there's the Order of the White Jacket. At the annual homecoming at the College of William and Mary in Virginia, you might see a famous governor, a college president, or any number of prominent business and professional people proudly wearing white jackets. The jackets signify that these men earned all or most of their way through college waiting on tables. They weren't ashamed of menial labor. They didn't hold out for the job they liked. They waited on tables. It helped them earn the education they have since put to such splendid use.

The Order of the White Jacket has a roster of which any group in the land could be proud. Perhaps there ought to be a chapter on every college campus in America. As long as it is honest, as long as it's dignified, there is no job that will not bring a number of fringe benefits beyond the money.

It's patience, it's perspiration, and it's persistence. I love the story of Thomas Edison. He worked on one invention for an awfully long time. In over 10,000 experiments, he had failed to produce an incandescent light. A young reporter asked him, "Mr. Edison, how does it feel to have failed over 10,000 times on one experiment?"

Edison looked at the young man and said, "Son, you're young; you're just getting started in life. I want you to know that I have not failed over 10,000 times on one experiment. I have successfully found 10,000 ways that would not work." He had to do 4,000 more experiments before he found a solution. It takes persistence. You aren't beaten until you quit.

If you look at the word *chump* carefully, take the U, and change it to an A, you change *chump* to *champ*. Over the long haul, that's really what I'm talking about.

We need to sell the idea of work. We need to sell the idea that you've got to get involved, that everything is not easy, that you've got to expend some effort on your part.

One of the greatest speeches ever made was one that Winston Churchill gave during those dark days of World War II.

The Allies were in full retreat. Dunkirk had been a disaster. The Nazi armies had swept all of Europe. They were sending Allied shipping to the bottom of the seas at a horrendous rate. Everybody was negative. Many religious leaders begged the free countries, England among them, to throw in the towel and save the needless bloodshed from what was obviously a hopeless cause.

Churchill delivered a famous speech. In his deep guttural voice, he said, "We shall fight on the beaches, we shall fight on the landing grounds, we shall fight in the fields and in the streets, we shall fight in the hills; we shall never surrender."

Not only did England survive, but with that speech, Churchill picked a nation up by its bootstraps, and the whole world was given hope. In the minds of many people, this was the turning point. He did not promise it would be easy, but he promised ultimate victory before they were through.

Probably the most famous speech that Churchill ever made after that one was made at the University of Missouri in Columbia. The introduction itself was so long that people grew restless and tired. When Churchill arose to speak, he stood silently for a moment and looked at the audience, and this was his speech:

"Never, never, never, never give up," and he held up the famous victory sign.

You can say it a lot of different ways, but ultimately, there are some things that we've got to do. If something is handed to us easily, often we do not appreciate it or use it. The great Greek orator Demosthenes was left a fortune by his father. But Greek law in those days required him to defend his inheritance in public debate. Demosthenes had a tremendous speech impediment. He was terribly shy and inhibited. He was humiliated and defeated in public debate, and he lost his inheritance.

But Demosthenes determined that he was going to learn to speak. He went down to the beach and put pebbles in his mouth. With those pebbles in his mouth, he started speaking into the waves and into the sea, and he became the most eloquent man in history. He became the greatest and most feared debater that the world perhaps has ever seen.

History doesn't even record the name of the man who grabbed his inheritance, but Demosthenes will live forever in the minds of those who put forth effort. With the right attitude and the right goals, persistence will move many obstacles. With the right objectives and attitude, persistence will save marriages, businesses, and schools.

Failure has often been described as the land of least persistence. If your job is harder than you wish, remember that you do not sharpen a razor on velvet. President Calvin Coolidge wrote, "Nothing in the world can take the place of persistence. Talent will not; nothing is more common than unsuccessful men with talent. Genius will not; unrewarded genius is almost a proverb. Education will not; the world is full of educated derelicts. Persistence and determination alone are omnnipotent."

Each rung of the ladder of success is designed to hold you just long enough for you to take the next step; it's not designed for you to sit down. The steps on the stairway to the top are designed to use as stepping stones and not as stopping stones.

When I was in school, I used to do a little boxing. I boxed just long enough to learn that it's a lot better if you talk about it than if you fight about it. That much I did learn. I love the story of James J. Jeffries, one of the great heavyweight champions of all time. He went into the ring for the heavyweight championship of the world with Jim Corbett.

Corbett won the first round, the second, and the third. As a matter of fact, Jim Corbett won twenty-three rounds, but Jeffries kept coming out. In the twenty-fourth round, James J. Jeffries knocked Jim Corbett out.

Vince Lombardi once said, "I've never known a man worth his salt who in the long run, deep down in his heart, did not appreciate the grind and the discipline." There is something in a good man that yearns for discipline. We need the discipline that simply says, "We've got to stay with it."

If you think I'm trying to sell you the concept of work, if you think I'm trying to promote the idea that it's fun to work and that the benefits that go with it are enormous, if you think I'm trying to talk you into enjoying your work and doing more, enthusiastically and with the right attitude, you're 100 percent right.

I have a chrome-plated pump, which I take to my talks. I've noticed something rather unusual: when I get aboard an aircraft carrying this pump, almost without exception I am the only passenger who has one. So I've got to assume that there is a shortage of chrome-plated pumps.

I believe that the pump is the story of your life, the story of America. I believe fervently that if you don't learn anything else from this book but the message of this pump, it will help you go where you want to go, do what you want to do, and be as you want to be.

A number of years ago, a couple of good friends of mine were down in south Alabama. It was a hot August day and they were riding around. It was terribly hot and they got thirsty. This was in the days before air-conditioned automobiles. They saw an old, abandoned farmhouse. Bernard Haygood was driving. He pulled behind an abandoned farmhouse and saw an old pump. He hopped out with his brother-in-law, Jimmy Glenn, and he ran over, grabbed the pump, and started to pump.

Bernard had been pumping a couple of minutes when he said, "Jimmy, you're going to have to get that old bucket over there and get some water out of the creek. We're going to have to prime the pump." This means that you've got to put some water in at the top before you can get some out.

Isn't this the story of life? Don't you know a lot of people who stand in front of the stove and say, "Stove, if you give me some heat, then I'll put some wood in you"? Don't you know a lot of secretaries who say, "Boss, give me a raise, and then I'll start coming to work on time"? How many times do we hear people say, "First of all, you reward me, and then I'll perform"?

It doesn't work that way. The farmer will tell you that before he can raise the crop, he's got to plant the seeds. Before he can reap the harvest, he's got to cultivate and irrigate the crop, or let the Lord irrigate it.

Bernard wanted that drink of water. He was thirsty. South Alabama does get awfully hot. He was pumping back and forth and up and down, and he was really working up a sweat.

The question invariably arises of just how much pumping you're willing to do in order to get a drink of water. Finally, Bernard said, "You know, Jimmy, I just don't believe there's any water down there."

"Yeah, there is, Bernard," said Jimmy. "You know, in south Alabama, the wells are deep. We're glad they are, because the deep wells are the ones that produce the good, clean, sweet, pure, best-tasting water of all."

Isn't this story telling us about life? The things that have value, the job that you really want—if everybody could qualify for them tomorrow, would they be of any value? Would the boy or the girl who would go out with anybody under any circumstances be considered a good catch? Isn't it true that the things that we have to work for are the things that really have value? Isn't it true that if we really want something badly enough—whether it's a new individual to sell our merchandise, a job, or the mate we're going to spend the rest of our life with—we've got to do a lot of working, a lot of persuading, and a lot of pumping to persuade them to our way of thinking?

Bernard wanted that drink of water. There were no two ways about it. He was thirsty, he was sweating, and he was pumping away, but again the inevitable question is going to arise: just how much pumping are you willing to do for one drink of water? Finally, Bernard threw his hands up in the air and said, "Jimmy," he said, "there just ain't any water down there."

"Bernard, don't quit," said Jimmy. "If you do, the water goes all the way back down, and then you're going to have to start all over."

Isn't this the story of life too? There's no way we can look at a pump and say, "Yep, two more strokes, and then I've got it." The water might be ten feet down; it might take an awful lot of pumping. But this we do know: if we pump long enough, hard enough, and enthusiastically enough, eventually it is going to bring forth the reward, which always follows the effort. Isn't that really the story of life?

And isn't it true, pumpers, that once you get that water flowing, all you've got to do is keep up a little easy, steady pressure, and you're going to have more water than you know what to do with? Sometimes you work and work, and nothing happens, then all of a sudden, you get a gusher.

Have you ever noticed that when things are good, they always get better, and when they're bad, they always get worse? It doesn't have anything to do with what's going on out there; it has to do with what's going on in your own mind. But this we know as surely as we know that the night follows the day: when you start something new, don't grab it casually, don't piddle around with it. Many people say, "Well, I'll piddle around and see what happens." Friend, you do it that way, and you're going to pump forever, and you are not going to get any water. But when you get that thing started, really give it a workout. When that water starts to flow, just keep up the steady pressure, and that's all you've got to do.

I love the story of the pump because it has nothing to do with your age or your education, with whether you're black or white, or Catholic or Jew or Protestant, with whether you're male or female, or educated or uneducated, whether you're introverted or extroverted, overweight or underweight. It has everything to do with your God-given rights as free people to work as long as you wish, as hard as you wish, and as enthusiastically as you wish to get everything in life that you really want.

Here you are. You've already moved up to step number five on our stairway to the top. Now I'll be the first to admit that you are perspiring freely, but you'll be the first to admit that you've got the biggest grin on your face that you've ever had. You're grinning because you've got the sweet satisfaction of knowing that through honest effort, labor, and production, you are climbing that stairway to the top, and you're getting to the step that takes you all the way to all of the things that are available in America today.

12

Desire and Intelligent Ignorance

In this chapter, we deal with desire and intelligent ignorance. Its purposes:

1. To fan your motivational flame to such an intensity that the hot water of mediocrity is converted to the steam of overwhelming desire.
2. To introduce you to intelligent ignorance and teach you how to take life's lemons and convert them to lemonade.
3. To show how to use obstacles as stepping stones to the richer life.
4. To sell you on free enterprise and the positive aspects of the America I love—to emphasize its strength, compassion, and goodness, with special attention reserved for the unique opportunities America offers you.
5. To identify the steps you can take to preserve and make America even stronger. It's because of this free-enterprise system that America is so tremendously important. Yes, I am one of those old-fashioned flag-waving Americans, and I'm proud of that fact.

This final segment involves step number six, which is the makeup step: the one that welcomes you as a success participator instead of a success spectator. If you've missed a step somewhere along the way, this one will enable you to catch up.

The ingredient that releases the power inside of you is desire. You see, when you flip the switch on the wall, you do not turn on the lights; you release the power that flows into the bulb: that's what turns on the light. You don't have to generate the electricity; all you've got to do is release the power.

Inside of you is an enormous amount of power, which only needs to be released. When you release the power, you really begin to move to the top. You begin to get to things that you really want out of the ball game of life.

When I talk about desire, I'm really talking about the ingredient that changes the hot water of mediocrity to the steam of outstanding success. Water at 211 degrees is hot. With it, you can shave or make a cup of coffee. But if you add just one more degree, you convert it to steam, and now you can propel a ship around the world or drive a locomotive all over the country.

Desire is the magic ingredient that moves individuals with average ability or intelligence to the top. They can become champion performers in everything they do.

Pete Gray, for my money, is a baseball immortal. When he was a very young man, he had an overwhelming desire. He said, "One of these days, I'm going to play major league ball. I'm going all the way to the big top. I'm going to play a game in Yankee Stadium."

Finally, in 1945, playing for the St. Louis Browns, Pete Gray made it all the way to the major leagues. He never hit a home run. He only lasted one year. He was not even a regular. But I fervently believe that Pete Gray is an immortal who belongs in the Baseball Hall of Fame, because Pete Gray made it all the way to the big top with just one good arm. Not once did he look down and say, "This I do not have." He kept looking up and saying, "This I do have." He did not let what he did not have keep him from using what he did have.

Success in life is not determined by having been dealt a good hand. It is determined by taking the hand you were dealt and utilizing it to the best of your ability. It's not your earning power that's the important thing; it's your yearning power. How badly do you want what you say you want?

Desire makes us winners. Desire takes an average individual, an average team, and enables them to win championships to go all the way to the top.

I'm not about to say that winning is everything, but I firmly believe that the effort to win is everything. I believe there's nothing in this world that equals the satisfaction of expending total effort to accomplish an objective.

I've gone into great detail about money because if we earn larger amounts of money, we can make bigger contributions and do more things for our fellow humans.

No, I don't believe winning is everything, but I do believe that the effort to win is. Nor do you have to choose between being a good winner and being a bad loser. Personally, I don't ever want to get enough experience at losing to be a good one. Knute Rockne, the immortal coach at Notre Dame, said, "If you give me eleven lousy losers, I'll give you a national championship football team," and I agree. Show me a good loser, and I'll show you a real loser.

I believe that desire creates intelligent ignorance. Intelligent ignorance means that you don't know what you can't do, so you go ahead and do it anyhow. In the sales world, we get a brand-new salesperson. They don't know anything about selling, the territory, procedure, or technique. But do they love the business? Do they love the product? Do they believe in what they are doing so they go out into sales not knowing what they can't do? They come in and win the top prizes over and over.

Everybody knows that aerodynamically, it is impossible for the bumblebee to fly. His body's too heavy. His wings are too light. Aerodynamically, it cannot be done, but the bumblebee doesn't read; the bumblebee flies. We frequently go ahead and do what we don't know we can't do.

I love the story of Henry Ford. He was not educated as an engineer, but one day, he had an idea. He said, "I'm going to build a V-8 engine." He called his engineers together and said, "Gentlemen, I want you to build a V-8 engine for me."

They looked at him as if the old man had lost his marbles. They said, "Mr. Ford, it's an engineering impossibility. It cannot be done."

Henry Ford said, "Gentlemen, you don't understand. We've got to have it now. Go build it."

The engineers went to work, came back shortly, and said, "It cannot be done."

Henry Ford said, "You don't understand. We've got to have it. Go build it."

They tried again, and for the third time, they came back and said, "Mr. Ford, it cannot be done."

"Gentlemen," he said, "apparently you do not understand. I must have a V-8 engine, and you must build it now, without any further delay. I say, go build the V-8 engine."

This time, the engineers built the V-8 engine—because one man said that it could and would be done.

Funny thing about intelligent ignorance: one person says it can't be done, and doesn't. Another person says it can be done, and does.

The "I can" philosophy is so significant that Mamie McCullough, a high-school teacher down in Thomasville, Georgia, had the idea of taking a can and having the students wrap it with paper. She clipped out some pictures of some eyes from magazines and pasted them on the can. The can became an "eye can." It was sitting on her desk, so every time the students looked up, they were reminded, "Eye can, eye can, eye can." When somebody said, "I can't," the rest of the class got all over him and said, "What do you mean you can't? You've got your eye can right in front of you."

With enough desire and enough intelligent ignorance, you can take a lemon and make lemonade. I love the story of General Creighton Abrams from World War II. General Abrams was completely encircled by the enemy. They were north, east, south and west. He called a staff meeting and said, "Gentlemen, for the first time in the history of this entire campaign, we can now attack the enemy in any direction." It's not the situation. It's the way we react to the situation that's extremely important.

Jacob Schick had a lemon. He was recuperating from an injury suffered while exploring for gold in Alaska and British Columbia in the early 1910s.

He wanted to shave, but the temperature in this sub-Arctic weather was forty degrees below zero, and the water froze as fast as he could get it out. You can't shave with a blade under those circumstances. Jacob Schick took his lemon, which was frozen water, and conceived of the electric razor. We see this happening over and over all the time, don't we?

In 1974, Neal Jeffrey was the quarterback for the Southwest Conference champion, the Baylor Bears. When he was a freshman, he was a stuttering third string quarterback. But he went to coach Grant Taeff and said, "Coach, I'm going to play first string football for you," and that's exactly what he ended up doing. As a matter of fact, he led the school to its first championship in some fifty years.

I love the story of Mike Weldon. As an infant, he was a sickly child. While in the hospital, he contracted polio. By the time he was sixteen, he was a paraplegic, confined to a wheelchair. When he was just twenty-one years old, he was fired from his job, where he had been earning $2.99 an hour as an engineering clerk. I don't know if you're aware of this or not, but twenty-one-year-old, unemployed paraplegics are not exactly in demand in the labor market. Let me tell you, however, what is in demand in any market in any time: dedicated people who enthusiastically believe that they are capable of doing a job and who are willing to do whatever is necessary to accomplish their objectives, so long as it's built on the right foundation of character, faith, loyalty, and integrity.

One month later, Mike Weldon got a job with Management Recruiters International, which, as I've noted, is the largest organization in the world for the placement of executive personnel. It was my privilege once to speak at a gathering of the organization, and I saw Mike Weldon in a wheelchair, receiving the award for the number one man in the entire company. Here was a young man with a limited education who was a paraplegic, but he did not look at his problems; he looked at the solution. You could say that Mike Weldon was given an entire sack full of lemons, so he ended up making a tub full of lemonade. As nearly as I can tell, it ended up being pink lemonade.

How badly do we want the things we say we want? Do we just wish for them? Years ago, I picked up a hitchhiker. For a long time, I've had a compulsion to motivate everybody I talk to in order to convince them to utilize their talents.

This young man and I were riding along. I started talking to him about success, positive thinking, optimism, and accomplishment. I ended by asking, "Son, how would you like to earn a lot of money and enjoy the good life?"

He had a faraway look in his eyes as he said, "Oh, I wouldn't mind."

That won't do it. It cannot be a casual thing. It must be something you really want. You must have the desire in order to take life's lemons and make lemonade. You're going to have frustrations, trials, disappointments, and defeat. This is an inevitable part of life itself, but we must have something to overcome those obstacles.

Charles Goodyear had a lemon: a prison sentence. While he was incarcerated, he could have moped and groaned and complained. But instead of just serving time, he made the time serve him: he discovered the process for vulcanizing rubber.

When Martin Luther was confined to Wartburg Castle for ten months, he translated the Bible into German. John Bunyan's prison sentence turned into *The Pilgrim's Progress*. It's not the situation; it's the way we react to it. And the way we react is largely determined by how badly we want to accomplish the things in life that we really want.

I love the story of Gene Tunney, one of the greatest heavyweight champions who ever stepped into the squared circle. Gene Tunney never would have been the heavyweight champion of the world if he had not broken both of his hands. As a young man, he was a light heavyweight. During World War I, fighting with the American Expeditionary Forces in France, he broke both of his hands. His trainer said to him, "Tunney, you'll never be the heavyweight champion. Your hands are too brittle." His doctor said to him, "These hands will not take the heavy pounding that punching demands."

Tunney started his boxing career as a puncher. He could knock a man out with either his left or his right. When those hands were broken, his doctor and trainer did not feel he could ever be the heavyweight champion, but he said, "Gentlemen, I'm going to be the heavyweight champion of the world. I'm going to learn how to box, and I'll win the championship."

History will tell you that when Tunney stepped into the squared circle with Jack Dempsey, he took the heavyweight championship on points. He had become one of the most skillful boxers ever to step into the ring. Experts will tell you that had Gene Tunney not broken his hands—had he tried to slug it out with Jack Dempsey—he never would have won. He took his lemon, which was two broken hands, and made his lemonade: the heavyweight championship of the world.

Preparing for his fight with Jack Dempsey, Tunney was obviously aware that Dempsey was a tremendous puncher, and he knew that he probably was going to get hit. He didn't think of this negatively; he thought of it realistically: you get in the ring with another man, there is no place to hide, so you're probably going to get hit.

How did Gene Tunney train? By running backwards. As a matter of fact, he ran backwards as much as he ran forward. Does this mean that he planned to retreat? Does this mean that he planned to fight a cowardly fight? Does this mean that he was afraid of Jack Dempsey? Not at all. He realistically faced the fact that he probably was going to get hit, and he planned in advance that if he did, he would instinctively move backward, out of the range of Dempsey's onslaught. He retained his championship title because of the way he trained: when Dempsey attacked him, Tunney skillfully backed up so he could regain his senses.

What I'm saying with these two stories is simply this: we know that things are going to happen to us, but we are not going to let temporary setbacks affect our overall career. We train, plan, and organize our efforts in such a way that we know where we're going, regardless of the circumstances.

Furthermore, I believe that if we are going to accomplish as much in the game of life as we would like, we must have the desire to help others

212 The Richer Life System

realize their objectives. I'd like to weave in one little story to show you how a simple conversation can affect others we associate with.

One day, I stepped aboard an aircraft with my chrome-plated pump, which I've already mentioned. A stewardess said to me, "What is that?"

I flippantly said, "It's a pump."

"What do you do with it?"

"I pump."

There is a plaque on it that says, "To Zig, America's Number One Flea Trainer." The stewardess asked, "Do you train fleas?"

"I certainly do."

"How do you train fleas?"

"I'll tell you what: when we're airborne, come over to my seat, and I'll explain to you how I train fleas."

Later she enthusiastically came to me and asked, "How do you train fleas?"

I explained to her that a flea trainer was an individual who jumps out of the jar, who is driven from within, who understands that you can get everything in life that you want if you will just help enough other people get what they want. I explained to her that a flea trainer does not tell others where to get off but shows them how to get on. I explained that a flea trainer does not try to see through people; a flea trainer tries to see people through. A flea trainer is not influenced by surrounding negative influences, but is motivated and driven from within. A flea trainer jumps out of the jar and removes those ceilings.

"For all of my life, I've wanted to be a stewardess," she replied. "I've only been one for a short period of time. It's been a miserable experience. Oh, it's not that I don't love my work, because I truly do. But my family has brought such unbelievable pressure to bear on me that I was about to quit today.

"As a matter of fact, they've made life so miserable every day of my life that today I have packed my bags. They are aboard this aircraft. This was to have been my last flight."

Then she straightened up perceptibly and said, "But I'm not going to quit. I love the work. I love being a stewardess. For me, it is right. For me, it is good. I'm going to stay with this. As a matter of fact," she said, "I'm going to be a flea trainer."

There was the trace of a tear in her eye as she leaned over, kissed me on the forehead, and walked away. I'll never forget it.

You can get everything in life that you want if you'll just help enough other people get what they want. Moreover, in order to get the things that we want, we've got to live and work in the free enterprise system. I never could have delivered this material in communist countries.

At this point, I would like to tell you one story that I personally believe involves every principle that I've been discussing.

Once I was speaking in Kansas City. I finished on Saturday afternoon, and it was too late to get back to my home in Columbia, South Carolina, that evening.

I was staying in the Muehlebach Hotel. I went upstairs to shower and change clothes. I came down, and as I stepped off the elevator, I heard the booming voice of a man whom I've come to love as a brother. You could have heard this voice for three blocks. He said, "Zig, where are you going?"

"Bernie," I said, "I'm going to dinner."

"I'll make you a deal. If you'll come and go with me, I'll buy."

I have a standard policy: when somebody offers to buy my dinner, I let them. So I said, "OK, Bernie, let's go."

We went to dinner, sat down, and we started to chat. We established a rapport that was almost instant because we had so many similarities all the way through our lives.

"Bernie," I said, "you've certainly come a long way to attend the sales rally."

"Yes, indeed. Am I ever glad that I did."

"You had to spend some bucks to get here."

"That's true," he said, "but really, Zig, I don't have to worry about money, thanks to my son, David."

"Bernie, that sound like a story."

"It is."

"Would you share it?"

"I'd be delighted to. You know, Zig, when our son was born, our joy knew no bounds. We already had our two daughters. Now that we had our son, the family was complete.

"But it wasn't very long before we realized that something was wrong. David's head hung too limply to the right side of his body. He drooled too much to be a normally healthy child.

"The family doctor assured us that he'd outgrow it. But we knew something was seriously wrong, so we took him to a specialist. Incredibly, the specialist diagnosed his condition as a version of club feet, and even treated him for that for several weeks.

"But we knew it was more serious than that. We took him to yet another specialist. After extensive examination, he said, 'This little boy is spastic. He has cerebral palsy. He's never going to be able to walk or talk or count to ten. I suggest that you put him in an institution for his own good and for the good of the normal members of the family.'"

When Bernie told me the story, he looked at me, and his dark eyes were flashing. He said, "But Zig, I'm not a buyer; I'm a seller. When this doctor said to me that I should consign my son to the life of a vegetable, I could not buy that idea, so I went to another doctor and another and yet another. Thirty different specialists in effect said, 'There is no hope for this little boy.'"

Then the Lofchicks heard of one more specialist, a Dr. Perlstein, down in Chicago, the foremost authority on cerebral palsy. Dr. Perlstein was booked over two years in advance with people from all over the world, but twelve days later, there was a cancellation, and they got an alternate appointment.

The family went down to Chicago, and Dr. Perlstein examined this little boy as no child has ever been examined before. He did a couple of things that were significantly different from what the other doctors had done. Each of them had simply taken the X-rays and the findings of the previous doctors, and all they did was agree with what the one before had said.

Dr. Perlstein started over. He took a brand-new set of X-rays. He called in the foremost authority on reading X-rays that was available and asked him to tell him what he saw. When he finished reading those X-rays, he went in to personally examine David. He told the Lofchicks, "This little boy is a spastic. He has cerebral palsy. He is never going to be able to walk or talk or count to ten, if you listen to the prophets of doom. But I want you to know that I am not problem-conscious, I am solution-conscious. I believe that if you are willing to do your part, something can be done for this little boy."

"Doctor, you name the price, and we'll pay it," said the Lofchicks. At that time, they could not easily afford a heavy financial burden.

The doctor spelled it out clearly: "You're going to have to push this little boy beyond all human endurance, and then you're going to have to push him some more. You're going to have to work him until he actually falls. Then you're going to have to work him some more.

"You've got to understand that once you have made your commitment, it is a forever commitment. If you ever stop, he will go back to where he was. You've got to understand that sometimes you're going to be working with him for months, maybe even years, before you can detect any progress. But if you stop, he goes all the way back."

The doctor said one more thing: "You must never let David take therapy in the presence of other victims of cerebral palsy because he will pick up their awkward, uncertain, unsure movements himself. You must not give him therapy with other victims."

The Lofchicks went home. They built a gymnasium down in the basement of their home. They hired a physical therapist and a bodybuilder, and they went to work. It took them several years, but finally one day little David Lofchick could move the limbs of his own body.

One day the therapist called Bernie and said, "I believe that David is ready. Why don't you come home and see?"

Bernie rushed home. David was down in the gymnasium on a mat, getting ready to do a push-up. As he started to rise into the air, the physical and emotional exertion was so great that there was not a dry inch of skin on that little body. The mat looked as if it had been sprinkled with water. Finally, when that one push-up was completed, mother and dad and David and the sisters and the neighbors, the therapist, the bodybuilder all broke down and shed tears. That clearly says that happiness is not pleasure; happiness is victory.

This story is even more remarkable when you understand that one of America's leading universities that examined this little boy, said there was no motor connection to the right side of his body. "He has no sense of balance," they said. "He'll have extreme difficulty ever learning to walk. He'll never be able to swim or skate or ride a bicycle."

Finally, my wife and I had the privilege of flying to Winnipeg, to attend the bar mitzvah of little David Lofchick. I wish that you could have witnessed what we did: this little boy walking tall and straight and strong to the front of the synagogue, saying the words that moved him into the faith of his forefathers. I wish you could have listened to him as he clearly and distinctly spoke those vows of his religious beliefs.

I wish you could see this little boy, who was supposedly never going to be able to walk, talk, or count to ten. He ran the wheels off of three bicycles before he started driving his own automobile. He skated on the neighborhood hockey team, did as many as a thousand push-ups in a single day, ran as much as six miles nonstop, and became one of the outstanding table tennis players in Winnipeg. As a seventh grader, he did extraordinarily well in ninth-grade mathematics. He grew into a man of 195 pounds, with a barrel for a chest. He shoots golf in the high eighties. He qualified for an unrated, ordinary $100,000 life insurance policy, which is the first and only time, to the best of our knowledge, that this has happened to a victim of cerebral palsy.

I saw this boy many times over the years, and I've often wondered how much bigger, faster, stronger, and smarter he would have been if he had

had the privilege of having a normal birth and a normally healthy body. A few years later, it dawned on me that had this boy been given more, he might well have ended up with less, maybe a great deal less.

The story of David Lofchick says everything that I've tried to say throughout this book. David Lofchick started working from a foundation that was extraordinarily solid. He had the advantage of having parents who not only loved him but saw him properly.

You're going to treat people as you see them. David's parents did not see him as a helpless, hopeless invalid. They looked at him as a baby and said, "Someday he is going to be a man, and he deserves his chance in life." You treat people as you see them, and they respond to the treatment. I'm convinced that that's why David was able to do so much.

Of all the families that I have ever seen in my life, there has never been one that has had more and bigger goals than the Lofchicks had for this little boy. They dreamed that their boy would have his chance in life. There were big goals, there were long-range goals, and there were daily goals. It was all put together in an attitude. Since this boy was about three years old, every day he was listening to motivational audio recordings as he was bathing, as he was taking therapy, as he was being taken to school. His whole attitude has been one of optimism and enthusiasm, and it's been pumped in ten thousand times: *I can, I can, I can*.

Let me tell you about David Lofchick. For one solid winter, with the wind chill hitting dozens of degrees below zero, David would set his alarm clock one full hour earlier than any other member of the family. He would get up, strap his skates on his feet, and crawl out to the frozen swimming pool. He spent one solid winter just learning how to stand up. Later, he skated on the neighborhood hockey team.

A person may say, "I only have twenty-four hours out of every day." Let me tell you how many hours David Lofchick has had all of his life: twenty-one. He's got to spend three hours every day just staying even, because if he doesn't spend those three hours staying even, he's got to back up.

I tell the story of David Lofchick in such detail because I believe it involves every principle that I've been talking about, with a super amount of a very special kind of love thrown in: the love that forgets self and aims it at the other person.

Hundreds of nights, when the Lofchicks were putting David to bed and were starting to put those braces on his legs, he would say, with tears streaming down his cheeks, "Can we leave them off just a night?" Or, "Can you leave them a little looser for just a night? Oh, please, mommy, don't tighten the braces tonight. Don't make me wear them."

If you are a parent, you know what I'm saying. How difficult it must have been to resist what he was requesting! But because they said no to the tears of the moment, they were able to say yes to the laughter of a lifetime. I'm convinced that that's what love really is all about.

This kind of love has to do with self-image. Today many parents do not discipline their children because they fear they will lose their approval and forget what is best for the child. I believe that's why God tells us in his book to thank him for everything, because before it happens, it has already crossed his desk. That makes it marvelous to know that we don't put the question mark after what God has put the period to.

Bernie Lofchick was in the world of sales and people development, but initially he did not have the financial resources to afford the enormous medical expenses that were involved. He had to work not only smarter but harder. This man, with an eighth-grade education, has one of the most brilliant minds I've ever encountered. He is the most completely educated uneducated man I have ever seen.

For seven solid years, Bernie Lofchick worked seven days and seven nights to acquire the wherewithal to give his son a chance in life. Today he is financially secure.

Let me emphasize that this story took place in Canada, where they also have the free enterprise system, which made this story possible. The free enterprise system enables us to get what we really want out of the game of life.

Throughout this book, I have emphasized how to build a healthy self-image, how to set and reach your goals, how to build an attitude foundation, the importance of work, and the value of having a happy relationship with your mate. I've stressed that the entire foundation for success is built on honesty, character, loyalty, faith, and integrity and that you cannot get something for nothing, because there ain't no free lunch. I've especially underscored that you can get everything in life that you want if you will just help enough other people get the things that they want.

Now I want to ask you an important question: if everybody in America were doing exactly the same thing that you are now doing, would our country be getting stronger, or would it be getting weaker? Only you and your conscience have the answer to that one. But it's my hope and belief that as you get excited and emotionally involved in a logical solution to this problem, you will, as one of the old commercials said, "give America your very best."

Throughout this book, I've been telling many stories. I tell stories because I believe that life itself is a story. There have been stories about people from every race, creed, and color. They come from all walks of life, and all sizes, shapes, and persuasions. Despite their obvious differences, all of these people have one thing in common: they all work, live, and believe in the free enterprise system that is the America that I love and the America that is strong and vibrant.

These people believe in the free enterprise system, so it's not hard for me to get excited about our system. The failure of communistic systems worldwide is well known. To paraphrase Winston Churchill, capitalism's problem is the uneven division of wealth; socialism's virtue is the even division of misery. They proudly boast that they are all equal, and it's absolutely true. They're all equally poor.

I'm disturbed by the number of people that buy the humanist approach. How many times have I heard somebody say, "I don't want to take Johnny to church. I don't want to force him to go, because that might turn him against it." Dr. Henry Brandt, a Christian psychologist, says that when people ask him whether they should force their children to go to church, he says, "Most definitely."

"Suppose it turns him against it?"

"Let me ask you a question. Have you ever had a sick child that you wanted to take to the doctor, but you would not because you feared it would turn the child against the doctor?"

The answer is obvious. As responsible people, you do what is best for the child. Dr. Brandt added, "The best thing to do is take the child to the church, because that's the place they need to be on Sunday and a lot of the other days as well."

We do what we know is best for the children. We do not let the dictates of a society that sometimes has abandoned its responsibilities tell us what we instinctively and inherently know is good for the child. It's really that simple.

We also know instinctively that there are some things that are not good for our country. We also know that we, as individuals, must begin to make our stand, and we must make it right now.

There are two groups of Americans who greatly concern me. One is the ostrich group. They say, "America has always come through. We have always solved our problems, and you can count on us: we will solve our problems now. Don't worry about it."

Two hundred years ago, Daniel Boone stood on a hillside in Kentucky with a rifle, killing passenger pigeons. He didn't shoot them, because that wasn't necessary. There were so many of them that he stood on a hillside and knocked them down with his rifle. According to the *World Book Encyclopedia*, one known flock of passenger pigeons was in excess of fifty miles wide and over 100 miles long. In this one flock of pigeons, there were over 250 million birds.

I can just hear somebody saying to old Daniel Boone, "Daniel, you'd better not kill those pigeons. We're going to run out one day."

Old Daniel would say, "You know, man, you're out of your mind. Look at all these the pigeons."

The last passenger pigeon died in the early twentieth century. There are none alive on the face of this earth today. Yet at one time, there was an enormous number of them all over this great land of ours.

I believe that the people who say, "don't worry about it" need to be told the story of Daniel Boone. Yes, we can lose everything that our ancestors and forefathers have worked for all of these years.

The other group that I'm concerned about in our great country is made up of the prophets of doom. They say, "What can I do? It's all over. It's too late. You can't fight city hall, big government, or bureaucrats. No, all politicians are crooked. What can one individual do?"

Let me simply say this: if my house were on fire, I would want somebody to tell me about it. But once that individual had told me, I would hope he would help me get a bucket of water and put it out.

My purpose here is to let you know that, yes, the house is on fire and to provide you with buckets of water. I fervently believe that the handwriting is on the wall for America, but I just as fervently believe that it is not indelibly imprinted on that wall. I believe with every fiber of my being that if we, as individuals, do what we know is right, if we take definite positive steps, we can erase the handwriting on the wall and write America's future more brilliantly, more beautifully, more gloriously than it ever has been written before.

We got in trouble because of the bullfrog theory. It's very simple: if you're going to boil a bullfrog, you don't throw him in boiling water. He'll pop out of there just as fast as you pop him in. You put him in cold water and turn the heat on. When the water begins to get warm, he lies there, stretches out a little, and says, "Man, that feels good. I like this warm bath. Never had one of these before. As a matter of fact, I'm so comfortable, I just think I'll take a little nap." Of course, we know the rest of the story. He wakes up dead.

The average twenty-five-year-old has watched television for approximately 25,000 hours, during which time they have seen 18,000 murders and witnessed tens of thousands of rapes and seductions. They have viewed and heard jillions of obscene and profane words. Is this what we can build a stable nation on? Is this what we build character on? You can probably remember advertising jingles from decades ago. Why? Because you heard them tens of thousands of times, until they became a part of you. Now think with me for a moment. If you have viewed 18,000 murders and tens of thousands of rapes and seduction, what are your thoughts going to be on? What kind of a character are we building among the youth of America today?

Adolf Hitler proved that people will believe anything if you tell it enthusiastically enough, often enough, and convincingly enough. Of course, the Bible told us that a long time ago, didn't it? As you sow, so also shall you reap.

A number of big lies have been going around in our country for a long time. Let me share these lies with you and how we have been fooled by them.

For decades, I have been told, "Ziglar, your generation was taught that sex was dirty." I would nod my head and say, "Yeah, that's right. That's what we were taught."

One day I got to thinking: is that what I was taught, or is that what I've been told I was taught? I started querying my peer group—not one or two or three, but dozens, from one end of the globe to the other. I would ask, "When you were a child, were you taught that sex was dirty? Think a moment before you answer."

In every case, without exception, they would say, "No, I wasn't taught that. When it was discussed, which wasn't very often, but when it was discussed, I was always told that it was sacred, that it was private, that it was between man and wife."

I thought about that a lot of times: sex is between man and wife; it's private; it's sacred. It's a beautiful relationship that goes beyond the mere procreation of the races. Now we're being told, "Since sex obviously is not dirty, it's all right. Go ahead: indulge in it with anyone. Of course, it should be in a meaningful relationship." People have bought it. As a result, for two generations we've had a tremendously tragic experience with pornography and illicit sex.

Big lie number two: poverty breeds crime. Of course, poverty does breed crime if every individual who's poverty-stricken is told over and over that poverty breeds crime. We are in effect saying, "Listen, friend, because poverty breeds crime, we'll understand if you go out and commit these crimes."

There's never been a definitive study that proved a correlation between poverty and crime. I am a child of the Depression. I can tell you with total certainty that jobs were tough. As a matter of fact, the unemployment rate was over 25 percent, in some areas even up to 50 percent. Yet the rate of crime was less in 1940 than it was in 1930. It was less going out of the Depression than it was going into the Depression. At the end of 1931, one of the toughest years, the crime rate was less than at the beginning. The same was true for 1935, the second toughest year of the Depression.

Saying that poverty breeds crime is a lie. Crime is the result of believing the wrong thing, being taught the wrong thing, failing to develop character, integrity, and honesty.

Big lie number three: people equal poverty. "We can prove it," they say. "Look at the poverty-stricken people of India." Is that a true case, or is it an isolated case? Let's look at some facts. Everybody's entitled to his own opinion, but nobody's entitled to the wrong facts. Population density in Holland is 50 percent greater than in India, and they have a very high standard of living. There are other factors. Africa has an extremely low density with abject poverty; America has low density and extreme wealth.

People have been so alarmed about the population explosion. People are saying, "We need a lower population; we need to reduce the number of babies." We really need more babies born to dedicated, concerned parents.

People say, "Kids cause problems, don't they?" You'd better believe they do if we as parents don't teach them honesty, honor, respect, loyalty, dignity, and faith. I feel that children are part of the solution and not part of the problem, provided we assume our responsibility of giving them loving discipline and care.

Yes, we do have some problems, but I am firmly convinced that we have solutions to those problems if we attack them head-on and get to the heart of the matter.

As our insurance friends are inclined to say, it's better to have it and not need it than to need it and not have it. When we have the strength, no nation on earth is going to attack us.

People say, "Where do we start? What do we do? What can I, as an individual, do? The world is such a cold, dark place, and so complicated now. I'm so young and useless, there's nothing I can do. But God, in all His wisdom, said, 'Just build a better you.'" and that's where you start.

There have been many civilizations since the beginning of time. Some grew quickly, some slowly. In every case, when they started to fall, they all failed in one generation, the reason was always the same, and the reason was a very simple one: the destruction of the family as a unit. America needs a reawakening and a rebirth of the family unit.

I believe that the James and Margaret Griffin family represent much of the good that is available in America today. For decades James drove a sanitation truck by day, worked in a steel mill by night, and had a couple of janitorial jobs. For over twenty years, he worked an average of twenty hours a day. James and Margaret started by buying two shares of stock. Over a period of years, they invested a little bit here and there until they had a nice home, completely furnished, as a result of the efforts that he expended over a period of years.

James took his vacations on Friday nights so he could go and watch his sons play football. Seven of his boys played football, and all of them were superior players. One of the sons, Archie, happened to be a better than average football player. To this day, he is the only man to have won two Heisman Trophies.

The next step is to accentuate the positive. We've got to start showcasing the progress, not just the problem. I think we then need to give people a progress report. If you tell me that I'm bad all the time, I'm going to try to be better, but if you say to me, "Ziglar, you're improving," that encourages me to do more. Let me give you a simple example.

One year, I was honored to speak at the Chamber of Commerce banquet in Yazoo City, Mississippi, where I was raised. This was a homeboy coming home. They invited me to speak at the high school the next day. They kept telling me about Gentle Ben Williams.

"Who's Gentle Ben Williams?" I asked.

"Mr. Ziglar, you must have been in a well somewhere. Gentle Ben Williams is the old conference middle guard at the University of Mississippi. He is a Yazoo City boy. They just elected him Colonel Rebel." He was the first African-American Ole Miss football player to earn All-America honors, drawing a first-team distinction in 1975.

I tell this story because Gentle Ben is a black man. I tell the story with such emphasis because thirteen years before, it took federal marshals to escort James Meredith onto the same University of Mississippi campus. Thirteen years before, they were saying, "Kill the black man." Thirteen years later, they were saying, "Elect him Colonel Rebel."

I'm not about to say that there's not prejudice still in existence. I'm not about to say that blacks have the same opportunities in all areas. But I do believe that in all fairness, we need to do some accentuation of the positive. I think we need to let the world know that there are more black millionaires in America than there are in the rest of the world combined. I think we need to let the world know that we have more blacks in American colleges than the rest of the world combined.

All I'm saying is that we are making progress. When you think about the development of the hottest, most sophisticated computer systems, when you think about advances in science and technology, you think about America.

Through it all, we must maintain our sense of humor and our tremendous enthusiasm, because people who have a sense of humor are not going to get uptight. They're going to work towards solving a problem.

If you think we've got problems today, let me remind you of what happened in 1858. America had a problem then. That was the year of the great whale oil shortage. Not only was there a shortage of whale oil, but leading experts the world over maintained that those dirty whales were not turning out the same caliber of whale oil that they had in the past. They said that our lamps would go down, our children would be uneducated, and we would raise them in a world of darkness. Then somebody discovered petroleum.

You've got to keep that sense of humor, because without it, we get in trouble. I love what Norman Vincent Peale says about problems: "The only people who don't have problems are in cemeteries."

Remember, out of every problem there comes an equivalent benefit. We also need to remember that running short of resources is not really the problem. It's not the lack of resources but the shortage of resourcefulness, as Dr. Billy Ray Cox of Harding University in Searcy, Arkansas, likes to say. He pointed out that 300 years ago, we were throwing coal at each other, because we used it only for a rock. He said that years ago, when they discovered oil on property, it was considered the black curse.

A few decades ago, there was no known use for uranium.

Did you know that they've figured out a way to take chicken droppings and run automobiles on them? Did you know that an automobile was driven all over Europe using water as the primary source of fuel? Do you realize that solar energy is coming into its own? And once we've really gotten busy and explored it, that we will, in fact, become entirely independent in supplying our oil?

I also believe that we've got to put our heroes back into our history books, because the spirit of America is caught as much as it is taught. We must have our kids daily reciting the Pledge of Allegiance and the American creed; we must fill their minds with the good, the clean, the pure, the powerful, and the positive; we must let the words of our immortal heroes ring down through the pages; we must let them hear Patrick Henry as he said, "Is life so dear, is peace so sweet, as to be purchased at the price of chains of slavery? Forbid it, Almighty God. I know not what course others may take, but as for me, give me liberty, or give me death." We need to hear the words of Nathan Hale, that twenty-one-year-old hero. As he stood in front of the hangman's gallows, they gave him a chance to capitulate and live a life of ease and luxury, but he said, "I regret that I have but one life to give for my country."

We need to put those heroes back into history books. We need to let John Paul Jones' words ring. When the British captain asked him if he was ready to surrender, he simply said, "I have just begun to fight." I believe that Americans all over have just begun to fight.

We need to identify with the bald eagle, which is our national symbol. We need to see the eagle flying high. We need to visualize him as he flies up in the air. From 5,000 feet, this national emblem of ours can look at the sun dead center and the next instant drop his eyes and spot a field mouse over a mile below.

That's the spirit of America, as far as I'm concerned, strong and powerful enough that we can spit in the teeth of the most powerful nations in the world and yet look down with compassion on the weaker nations and those that are oppressed and say, "We are with you. We're concerned about you, and we want to do something for and about you." Yes, we need to have our heroes back in our history books.

Now I would like to take you on a trip across this beautiful America that I'm so much in love with. I'd like you, if you will, to get aboard a jet airliner with me, down in Dallas. Now as we fly westward, we're going to look down on El Paso, the home of Lee Trevino, who is of Mexican ancestry. When he was a child, he was thrown off some country club courses. Later those very courses that threw him off were delighted to invite Lee back. You see Lee rising from his foundation, rising above his environment; because he lived in America, he has been an enormous success.

Let's leave from there. We head north, over the Grand Canyon. I think you should see it from there. It's a magnificent sight. Let's stop in on Carlsbad Caverns. I think everybody ought to see them. Now let's go westward and fly across the Mojave Desert. Almost immediately after we leave the desert, we see humans have added water, and we find the fields of California and their tremendous productivity.

Let's land in Los Angeles, the home of a man named Carl Karcher. Carl—a big guy, six feet four inches tall, weighing 240 pounds—was an eighth-grade dropout. He believed in the free enterprise system. He bet on himself by pledging his net worth to get the capital investment necessary to become an entrepreneur. Now that, ladies and gentlemen, just means he hocked his 1941 Plymouth for $326 so he could buy a hot dog stand, but he made a good hot dog. People bought them. He treated them like nice people, and they responded. He bought another little hotdog stand. Today Carl's Jr. restaurants are a major nationwide chain.

Let's go from there to San Mateo, California, home of a man named Robert Patchin. He has sold real estate for many years, even though he has never seen a home, because he is completely blind. Here's a blind man who saw the greatness of America, who saw the opportunity that we have. Because he lives and works in this free enterprise system, he has been able to provide for his family and contribute to his community and America itself.

Let's go north now. I just want to take a little sightseeing trip. I think you ought to see the sequoias and the redwoods. I think you want to turn and fly over the magnificent Rocky Mountains. What a spectacle they make from the air! Let's fly across the wheat fields of Kansas and Nebraska, and let's look down in Chicago, at a man named Bill Branum, a World War II veteran, who started selling encyclopedias for World Book door-to-door and became a chief executive officer and chairman of the board. He started from absolute zero, from a belief in the free enterprise system, convinced that if he knocked on enough doors and talked to enough people, things would happen.

Let's leave Chicago and fly slightly north to land in the little community of Ada, Michigan, the headquarters of the Amway Corporation. In 1957, two young veterans started a business in a converted service station until it became a worldwide organization. The two men who started this company, Jay Van Andel and Rich DeVos, had the attitude of gratitude, because they were unquestionably the most vocal exponents of the free enterprise system. In Ada, they established the Center for Free enterprise at a cost of hundreds of thousands of dollars in order to pass on to coming generations what this is all about.

We leave Ada and go down to Detroit. This time, I would like for us to stop and attend a banquet. I want us to meet a little lady there whose name is Ola Zimmerman. I was with her some years ago at an awards banquet, where she was recognized as the outstanding real estate salesperson in the entire area of Detroit. As I talked with Ola, I discovered that she had escaped from her native land at night, hungry, living on roots and berries to get out of an oppressive communistic system and come to America. As I talked with her, I had to listen very carefully, because she spoke in a guttural accent that is very difficult to understand. But as I listened to Ola, it became immediately obvious why she was able to sell so tremendously effectively, because, you see, Ola Zimmerman did not sell a house on a lot. She sold a home on a little piece of America.

I wish you could talk to more immigrants, so please come go with me. Let's fly over the beautiful grasslands of Kentucky and look down on the magnificent hillsides of Tennessee. Let's look down for a moment on Nashville and meet Sam Moore. Sam Moore is quite a guy: years ago, he immigrated to America from Lebanon. Someone over there told him about America, told him about the Lord, and said, "This is where you really ought to be." He arrived here penniless, got a job in a service station, then discovered he could make 15 cents an hour more scrubbing floors in a grocery store. Then he responded to an ad to sell Bibles door-to-door. Sam became a very comfortable man financially as the chairman of the board and chief executive officer for the Thomas Nelson Publishing Company. I wish you could listen to him tell you with tears in his eyes and gratitude in his heart what he thinks about America and what the free enterprise system is all about.

From Nashville, we fly across the steel mills of Birmingham. We look down, and we know this is responsible for part of the affluence that is America. We stop in Montgomery, the home of a little lady who had sore feet. This lady's name is Rosa Parks. Once she sat down in the wrong section of the bus. The bus driver told her to move, but Rosa's feet hurt and she refused to stand up and move to the back. Because she refused to stand, an entire people stand taller, Martin Luther King gave birth to a dream, and a million feet marched. As a result of that, civil rights legislation came into being, because we realized for the first time that the system had not been dealing with our black brothers and sisters as fairly as it should. Many doors were opened, and many people discovered for the first time that the color of the skin had nothing to do with the heart and the ability inside.

We're going to leave Montgomery to fly down to Pensacola, Florida, the home of Daniel James. His mother finished high school, but she was not content with the black schools in Pensacola, so she started her own school and put Daniel in it along with sixty other students, charging them a nickel a day (when they could come up with a nickel). She taught them love, honesty, loyalty, faith, integrity, and stick-to-it-iveness. She taught them patriotism; she taught them to love America. Later, Daniel James became much better known as General Chappie James, head of the North American Air Defense Command. He was given the eleventh commandment by his mother: "Thou shalt not quit, and thou shalt make certain that your children get a better education than you get."

Leaving Pensacola, we're going to fly westward, across New Orleans, where for the first time our country gained international respect. Andrew Jackson and his coonskin heroes didn't exactly look like heroes to a lot of people. But when they withstood the British onslaught at New Orleans, the civilized world knew that they'd better take another look at this little land called America.

We're going to leave New Orleans and go over for our final stop in Waco, Texas, the home of Braz Walker, the author of books about tropical fish.

Braz Walker knew more about tropical fish than almost anybody in this country, but he is not the usual American success story. At age nineteen, he was inflicted with bulbar polio, and after that time, he spent twenty-four hours out of every day in an iron lung. The only part of his body that was functional was his mind and his tongue. As he lay on his back, he typed his own manuscripts with the aid of a special device rigged for him by General Electric.

I could tell you a lot of other stories—thousands and thousands of them. But in the final analysis, all of them say the same thing: "Because we live in, love, and work in the free enterprise system that is America, we can do things that no other people on the face of this earth can do."

If it sounds as if I'm in love with my country, I plead guilty. If it sounds as if I love the free enterprise system, I plead guilty. There is no other nation on the face of this earth that even comes close to what America has to offer. We're a land that's wealthy, it's true, but we're also a land of compassion. Whether it's a local situation or an earthquake in Chile, whether it's a disaster in Guatemala, whether it's a typhoon in Korea, or famine in Biafra, it doesn't make any difference. When you get there, you will see more Americans with American goods rendering American aid than all of the rest of the world combined.

Our land is not perfect, but it is the greatest. If you want to be on a winning team, I'm going to urge you to join America. I'm convinced that this is still the land of the free. I'm convinced that this is still the home of the brave. I'm convinced that this is still the land where any man or any woman can get anything they really want, provided they are willing to do their part.

The purpose of this book has been to get you into action, and anything less is unacceptable to me. I certainly hope that it is unacceptable to you, because you are the only person on the face of this earth who can use your ability. It's an awesome responsibility. I believe you were designed for accomplishment, engineered for success, and endowed with the seeds of greatness, but we've got to put it to work.

Webster's Dictionary defines *opportunity* as a fit time. And I believe that now truly is a fit time for you. The information and inspiration in this book will enable you to go where you want to go, do what you want to do, and be what you want to be. I say this without boasting because this information has been gleaned from some of the wisest men that this country and this world have ever produced.

In reality, all I've been doing is serving as a reporter, bringing to you the good news that has been accumulated over a period of years. Of infinitely more importance, I've drawn on the infallible wisdom of Almighty God and what he has said in his book.

I'd like to also assure you that if I were on trial for my life and you were my judge and my jury, and I had been instructed to produce something for you that would enable you to get the most out of the game of life, I would have presented this material exactly as I have done.

Now that I've shared these thoughts on how to reap richer rewards from this life, let me urge you to follow the admonition in Matthew's Gospel: "But seek ye first the kingdom of God and his righteousness, and all these things shall be added unto you. . . . For what is a man profited, if he shall gain the whole world, and lose his own soul?" (Matthew 6:33, 16:26)

You are you, and you now know there never has been and there never will be another you. You know that you are created in God's image, only slightly less than the angels, and you know that's true about others as well.

You never look down on or up to anyone. You understand that no one can make you feel inferior without your permission, which you now refuse to give to anyone. You know that you can get everything in life that you want if you'll just help enough other people get what they want. You also understand that ability can take you to the top, but it takes character to keep you there, and that while there's plenty of room at the top, there is not enough room to sit down.

This is the beginning of a new way of life, which demonstrates that happiness isn't pleasure; it's victory. Perhaps most importantly, you know that the beginning must always remain the beginning, because success and happiness are not destinations. They're exciting, never-ending jour-neys. You are in the position of being a go-getter, and you're beginning to be a go-giver.

I say welcome to the beginning and goodbye to the old you and the old way of life. Today many people end a visit or a phone call by saying, "Have a good day." That's nice, but I believe life has considerably more to offer than just a good day. I believe that if you believe in yourself, your fellow humans, your country, what you're doing, and Almighty God, your good days will extend into a good forever, and I truly will see you at the top.

CPSIA information can be obtained
at www.ICGtesting.com
Printed in the USA
JSHW021525261221
21490JS00003B/3

9 781722 505127